Commemorative Issue

14th Annual Tournament
1957 - 1970

U. S. National Senior Open

PLAYED IN HONOR OF

Walter Hagen

The Immortal "Haig"

A Pictorial History of Golf

A Pictorial History of Golf

Nevin H. Gibson

South Brunswick
New York: A. S. Barnes and Company
London: Thomas Yoseloff Ltd

A. S. Barnes and Co., Inc.
Cranbury, New Jersey 08512

Thomas Yoseloff Ltd
18 Charing Cross Road
London W.C. 2, England

6770
Printed in the United States of America

This book is affectionately dedicated to Walter C. Hagen. No one individual has contributed more to professional golf than he has. His unmatched record of eleven major titles is exceeded only by his colorful golfing career. His great sportsman-like qualities have made an indelible mark upon the golfing world. Every professional golfer today owes a word of thanks to Walter Hagen. His endeavor to elevate the status quo of professional golf has succeeded far beyond the expectations of his contemporaries.

Preface

"To write the history of golf as it should be done," wrote Andrew Lang in 1890, "demands a thorough study of all Scottish Acts of Parliament, Kirk Sessions records, memoirs and in fact of Scottish literature, legislation, and history from the beginning of time. . . . A young man must do it, and he will be so ancient before he finishes the toil he will scarcely see the flag on the short hole at St. Andrews from the tee."[1]

The above statement was made some 80 years ago, before golf expanded throughout the world. It was most difficult to conceive of the vast amount of work which would be required to write such a history at this time.

In 1921, Fred R. Barnard coined the phrase, *"One Photo Is Worth A Thousand Words."* In many aspects, this claim is not too farfetched. All illustrations, whether photographed, painted, or drawn, offer many values to an observer — particularly in the field of outdoor sports. By such standards, the compiler has endeavored to present herewith, *A Pictorial History of Golf,* supplemented with explanations and quotes from over 100 other golf books and magazines.

Acknowledgments

The compilation of this volume was a project which exceeded the time allotted and provided numerous obstacles, many of which became insurmountable. Although it was a labor of love, it was finally completed only through the valuable assistance I received from many other people and golfing associations. And it is to these most responsive and dedicated individuals and organizations that I wish to express my most sincere appreciation for making possible this FIRST and ONLY *Pictorial History of Golf.*

Firestone Golf and Country Club, Akron, Ohio
United States Golf Association, Golf House, New York
Professional Golfers Association of America, West Palm Beach, Fla.
Golf World Magazine, Southern Pines, N. C.
The Royal and Ancient Golf Club of St. Andrews, Scotland
The Western Golf Association, Golf, Illinois
The Prestwick Golf Club, Scotland
Doral Hotel and Country Club, Miami, Florida
The National Golf Foundation, Chicago Illinois
The Royal Liverpool Golf Club, England
Augusta National Golf Club, Augusta, Georgia
The Royal Blackheath Golf Club, London, England
Dunlop Sporting Division, New York

Golf Digest Magazine, Norwalk, Connecticut
Bing Crosby Clam-bake, Pebble Beach, California
The McGregor Company, Cincinnati, Ohio
Wilson Sporting Goods, Chicago, Illinois
A. G. Spalding Company, Massachusetts

And to the following individuals:

Bertram Eary, London, England
Max Elbin, Washington, D. C.
Clifford Roberts, Augusta, Ga.
Herb Graffis, Ft. Lauderdale, Fla.
Will Grimsley, New York, N. Y.
Cathi Taylor, Miami, Fla.
Marshall Dann, Golf, Ill.
Joe Gambetese, Washington, D. C.
Dave Eisenberg, New York, N. Y.
Bud Harvey, Palm Beach, Fla.
Madman Morris, Tampa, Fla.
Billy Casper, California
Jack Level, Elmhurst, N. Y.
Dick Taylor, Southern Pines, N. C.
Deane Beman, Washington, D. C.
Charlie Price, New York, N. Y.
Robert T. Greasey, Palm Beach, Fla.
Bing Crosby, Pebble Beach, California
Bruce Koch, Rochester, N. Y.
Cecil Leitch, London, England
Chick Evans, Golf, Ill.
Gene Sarazen, Germantown, N. Y.
George Zaharias, Tampa, Fla.

Philip R. Wahl, Augusta, Ga.
Patricia Cushman, Palm Beach, Fla.
Tom Tully, Chicago, Ill.
James D. Dean, Cincinnati, Ohio
Mrs. Gwenn Graham, Pebble Beach, Calif.
Harry C. Eckhoff, Chicago, Ill.
R. Otto Probst, South Bend, Indiana
William A. Booe, Palm Beach, Fla.
Willie Hunter, Los Angeles, California
Joe C. Dey, Jr., New York, N. Y.
Arnold Palmer, Latrobe, Pa.
Paul MacDonald, New York, N. Y.
R. Dean English, Akron, Ohio
George Arble, Washington, D. C.
Frank Hannigan, New York, N. Y.
Robert Trent Jones, New York, N. Y.
Jackie Gleason, Miami, Fla.
Lillian Harlow, Southern Pines, N. C.

Robert T. Jones, Jr., Atlanta, Ga.
Frank Strafaci, Miami, Fla.
Robert D. Gibson, Washington, D. C.
Michael J. Connor, Akron, Ohio

And to the many others who, inadvertly, may have been omitted from the above list. My apologies for these omissions.

And to those who have departed to greener fairways:

The late, David Scott Chisholm
The late, D. M. Mathieson
The late, Tony Lema
The late, Ed Dudley
The late, Grantland Rice
The late, Robert E. Harlow
The late, Horton Smith

Contents

The Origin of Golf?

When Caledonia, stern and wild,
Was still a poor unkilted child,
Two simple shepherds clad in skins,
Finding that dulness day by day,
Grew irksome, felt a wish to play.
But where the game? In those dark ages
They couldn't toss — they had no wages.
Till one, the brighter of the two,
Hit on a something he could do.
He hit a pebble with his crook,
And sent the stone across a brook;
The other, tempted then to strike,
With equal ardour 'played the like,'
And thus they went with heart and soul
Toward a distance quarry hole,
With new success contented.
'Twas thus the prehistoric Scot
Did wonders by an idle shot,
and golf was first invented.

By an anonymous writer
From the *Golf Book of East Lothian*[2]

A Pictorial History of Golf

1

The Beginning to 1900

By virtue of its age and its royal approval, golf is commonly referred to as the Royal and Ancient Sport. The origin of golf is unknown. Centuries ago, golf was a popular amusement in St. Andrews, Scotland, and many historians claim that St. Andrews is the cradle of golf. There is evidence that golf was a popular amusement in St. Andrews in 1413, when the university was formed, but its origin is unknown though it is generally conceded by all that the game commenced in Scotland. The oldest written evidence concerning the game establishes the origin to be in Scotland, and there exist no authenticated documents which contradict this theory.

Scotland's initiative in organizing golfing societies and clubs to a degree of recognized proficiency obviously elevated the social aspects of the game and, by the same token, stimulated an increased interest among her own populace. This interest later expanded to England. These organizations possessed influential political powers which aided them in obtaining civil recognition. This recognition materially aided them in receiving land grants for their links and other facilities. The membership of these golfing societies and clubs was confined to a privileged group, a clientele referred to as "Gentlemen Golfers." These organizations carried a considerable amount of prestige.[3]

The following early accounts are quoted as a matter of interest and are the first written evidence on the game of golf that we know of today. It describes golf's progress in Scotalnd from the time it was a "forbidden, disgraceful recreation," to the period when it became a "legal, honorable, and respectful sport."

Golf was prohibited in 1457 by the Scot's Parliament of King James II. An extract of the decree, dated March 6, read in part: . . . "and that Futeball and Golfe be utterly cryed downe and not be used." Golf, it seems, began to interfere with compulsory archery training to such an extent that it necessitated the sovereign to issue this proclamation for the common defense of the country. During this period, the bow was the principal weapon of defense. Scotland and England were noted for their superiority in mastering this weapon, particularly England, which at times was not on the friendliest terms with Scotland.

In 1471 an act was passed by the parliament under the regime of James III forbidding golf. This act read in part: "Futeball and Golfe be abused in time cumming," with further mention that it interfered with essential archery training.

Twenty years later it was ordained under the acts of James IV that neither golf nor other unprofitable sport be played as it interfered with the more important duties. However, in spite of these proclamations, issued under the reign of three different regimes, golf continued to be a popular amusement in Scotland.[4]

FEAST OF ST. NICHOLAS
Home of a cobbler in Holland. Painted by Jan Steen 1626–1679. Boy in center with golf club and ball which from all indications appear to be authentic in every respect. (This painting was discovered by H.S.C. Everard in the Rotterdam Gallery in 1902. Mr. Everard wrote the book, *The History of the Royal and Ancient Golf Club of St. Andrews* in 1907, William Blackwood & Sons) (Photo by courtesy of the late D. Scot Chisholm)

THE SABBATH BREAKERS
During the sixteenth century when golf was a forbidden pastime on Sundays. (Photo by courtesy of the Fine Art Society, London, England)

King Charles I, receiving a letter delivered to his hands while playing on the links of Leith, located near Edinburgh, Scotland. This letter gave him the first accord of the resurrection and rebellion in Ireland. After reading the message, he suddenly called for his coach and, leaning on one of his attendents, and in great agitation, drove to the Palace of Holyrood house, from whence next day he set out for London. King Charles was extremely fond of the game and played it during his confinement at Newcastle when it was occupied by the Scots about 1640-1641. (Photo by courtesy of Tom Auchterlonie, St. Andrews, Scotland). Caption from James Lindsay Stewart, *Golfiana Misecllanea.* Hamilton, Adams & Co., 1887.

According to the Royal Financial Account, the king violated his own act when he played golf with the Earl of Bothwell from 1503 to about 1506.

One century later the situation remained the same, but the people continued to play golf. In 1592 the Town Council of Edinburgh prohibited the playing of golf on Sundays. The next year, the same Council issued a similar act, this time specifying "during devine services," and imposing a forty-shilling fine for violations. These later acts were obviously instigated by church officials since early accounts reflect that a large number of church members were fined and sentenced for participating in golf during the time of sermons. In some cases church ministers were also offenders and were promptly deposed from office.[5]

When the invention of gunpowder superseded the bow as a practical weapon of war the statutes prohibiting the playing of golf became obsolete. In 1603 King James VI appointed William Mayne as Club-maker, and, in 1618, James Melvill as Ball-maker.[6]

The first known act permitting golf came in 1618, when the king authorized and encouraged the playing of golf on Sundays with the stipulation that "devine services must first be attended."

In 1633, King Charles I ratified a previous act and "commanded" that his loyal and dutiful people should not be molested in their "lawful" recreations after having first done their "duty to God."[7]

Approximately one century after golf became legal, Scotland organized the first golfing society. The Honorable Company of Edinburgh Golfers was established in 1744, during which year the club held its first annual tournament. This Golfing Society used the famous links of Leith near Edinburgh and survived until 1831, when it ceased operations. In 1836 this club was reactivated, this time using the Musselburgh links.[8]

In 1754, the St. Andrews Society of Golfers, now known as the Royal and Ancient Golf Club, came into existence. This club has been in continuous operation since activation. This, combined with other circumstances, obviously contributed to the recognition of the Royal and Ancient Golf Club as the leading golf club and the foremost authority on golf.[9]

Golf was played at Blackheath, near London, in 1608. There is, however, no written evidence which substantiates the existence of an organized golf club before 1778.[10]

In 1761, the Bruntsfield Golf Club was established. This club, like many others, lost its original records.[11]

The years following, during the eighteenth century, the following golf clubs and societies were es-

THE CRADLE OF GOLF
Royal and Ancient Golf Club 1798
A rare old sketch of St. Andrews Golf Club depicting a group of golfers on the first green in 1798. The Royal and Ancient Golf Club was established in 1754 and is the oldest golf club in the world which has remained in continued existence. It is the spiritual home of all golfers and its rules of play are observed world-wide. (Photo by courtesy of Jack Level, Elmhurst, L.I., N.Y.) Caption from H.S.C. Exerard, *The Royal & Ancient Golf Club*, Wm., Blackwood & Sons, 1907.

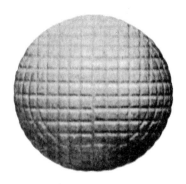

Old leather ball, "Feathery," on left was made by William Gourlay, famed ball maker, up until 1848. The hand-hammered gutty, in center, was used from 1848 to about 1851; then the machine-marked gutty was used up until 1902. Doctor Coburn Haskell, a dentist from Cleveland, Ohio, invented the rubber ball which is used today.

tablished: the Edinburgh Burgess Golf Society in 1773;[12] the Musselburgh Golf Club in 1774;[13] the Crail Golfing Society in 1786;[14] the Aberdeen Golf Club in 1780;[15] The Glasgow Golf Club in 1787;[16] The Bruntisland Golf Club in 1797.[17]

During the first half of the nineteenth century approximately 30 golf clubs were instituted. Some of these soon disbanded while others became very prominent. Some of the more famous and the year of their inception, follow: Royal Albert (Montrose) Golf Club, 1810;[18] Innerleven Golf Club, 1820; Royal Perth Golfing Society, 1824;[19] North Berwick Golf Club, 1832;[20] Carnoustie Golf Club, 1839; Leven Thistle Golf Club, 1846; Inverness Golf Club, 1847;[21] Prestwick and Prestwick St. Nicholas Golf Club, 1851;[22] Pau Golf Club, (France), 1856; and King James VI Golf Club, 1858.[23]

The decade of the 1850's is one of the most interesting and important in the history of golf. Although the game existed some four centuries prior to 1850, its progress was slow until then. One of the principal forces in golf's progress was the St. Andrews Golf Club. In 1854 the stone-gray clubhouse, which still stands, was completed, and the club assumed its new title — The Royal and Ancient Golf Club of St. Andrews — which King William IV had conferred in 1834.[24] St. Andrews, Scotland, is recognized as the world's golfing embassy and the St. Andrews Golf Club is the spiritual home of all golfers.[25]

During the 1850's Hugh Lyon Playfair, the town provost, exerted every effort to make St. Andrews attractive. He drew the citizens, while Allan Robertson, the first noted professional golfer, drew the golfers. This combination stimulated great interest in the game.[26] Allan Robertson, reputed as the greatest professional golfer during the 1850's, was the first to score a 79 over the St. Andrews Course.[27]

In 1855 there was but one course at St. Andrews, and the same nine holes served for the outward as for the inward play. Each hole was marked by a small iron pin, with a bit of red rag attached. The greens were in the "rough," and the bunkers were their natural state.[28]

The golfing enthusiasm prevailing at St. Andrews even before the 1850's is described in the famous poem written by George F. Carnegie in 1833. The poem is as follows:[29]

ADDRESS TO ST. ANDREWS

St. Andrews! they say that thy glories are gone,
That thy streets are deserted, thy castles o'erthrown:
If thy glories be gone, they are only methinks,
As it were, by enchantment, transferred to thy Links.

Though thy streets be not now, as of yore, full of prelates,
Of abbots and monks, and of hot-headed zealots,
Let none judge us rashly, or blame us as scoffers,
When we say that instead there are Links full of Golfers,
With more good heart and good feeling among them,
Than the abbots, the monks, and the zealots who sung them.

We have red coats and bonnets, we've putters and clubs;
The green has its bunkers, its hazards, and rubs;
At the long hole across we have biscuits and beer,
And the Hebes who sell it give zest to the cheer:

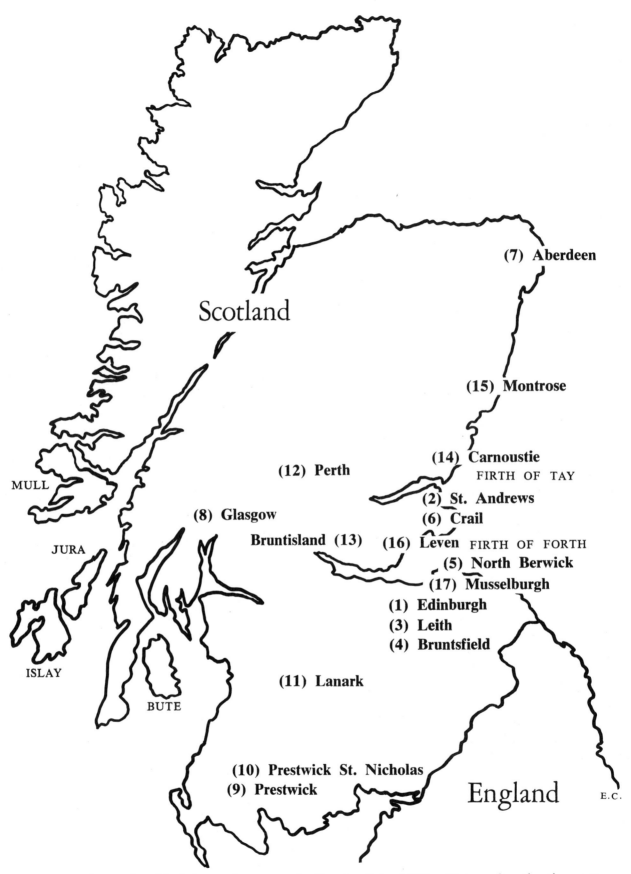

A GEOGRAPHIC VIEW OF SCOTLAND'S GOLF CLUBS IN 1852

Locations of golf clubs and courses in Scotland in 1852. Dates of activation are as follows: (1) 1744, (2) 1754, (3) Home course of (1), (4) 1761, (5) 1832, (6) 1786, (7) 1780, (8) 1787, (9) 1851, (10) 1851, (11) 1851, (12) 1824, (13) 1797, (14) 1839, (15) 1810, (16) 1846, and (17) 1774.

Posed above are the leading professional golfers of the world during the 1850's at the Royal and Ancient Golf Club of St. Andrews, Scotland. From *left to right* are: James Wilson, caddie and Clubmaker, Bob Andrews (The Rook), Willie Dunn, Willie Park, Alan Robertson, Old 'Daw' Anderson, Tom Morris and Bob Kirk. (Photo by courtesy of D. Scott Chisholm)

If this make not up for the pomp and the splendor,
Of mitres, and murders, and mass — we'll surrender;
If Golfers and caddies be not better neighbors,
Than abbots and soldiers, with crosses and sabres,
Let such fancies remain with the fool who so thinks,
While we toast old St. Andrews, its Golfers and Links.

George Fulletron Carnegie was born in 1799 and died at Montrose in 1843. The above poem was his most famous which was published in the book *Golfiana* in 1842 at Edinburgh, one year before he died.

Another contributing factor to golf's rapid ex-pansion in the 1850's was the revolution in the golf-ball industry. Prior to 1848 golf balls were known as "Featheries." They consisted of a small spheroid of leather stuffed with approximately one top hat of feathers. The leather was cut into three small pieces and sewn together with waxed thread, leaving a small pin hole in which the feathers were inserted with a stuffing iron. This method was tedious and slow. One man could make approxi-mately four balls per day. In 1848 there was a vast improvement in the golf ball with the introduction of "gutta percha." Gutta percha is a resin or gum

SIR HUGH LYON PLAYFAIR
The Lord Provost of St. Andrews, who was instrumental in its
progress during the 1850's. Sir Hugh drew the citizens and Al-
lan Robertson, the noted professional, attracted the golfers. Sir
Hugh Playfair was the captain of the Royal and Ancient Golf
Club in 1956. (Portrait by courtesy of the Royal and Ancient
Golf Club of St. Andrews)

Mr. Hay Wemyss. captain of the Royal and Ancient Golf Club of St. Andrews in 1854, preparing to drive. From left to right are Tom Morris, Mathew Gorm, a caddie, Mr. Robert Cathcart, Old Daw, a caddie, a spectator, Boy Jamie Anderson, son of Old Daw and who later on won three consecutive British Open championships, Allan Robertson, Mr. Wallace. (Photo by courtesy of the Royal & Ancient Golf Club of St. Andrews.) Caption from Sandy Herd, *My Golfing Life*, Chapman & Hall, Ltd., 1923.

from certain types of Malayan trees of the sapodilla family. It resembles rubber but contains more resin. These new balls were simple to make and their cost far more reasonable. They were durable, more accurate, carried a longer distance, and responded more favorably in the wind.[30] The professionals, who detested the introduction of the "gutties," were finally converted shortly afterwards.[31] The first gutta-percha ball was made in 1845 by the Rev. Dr. Robert Adams Patterson from this substance which was used as a protective packing for certain items shipped from India to England.

In 1844, Allan Robertson, St. Andrews professional, turned out 2456 featheries.[32]

In 1857 the first National Golf Club Championship was held at St. Andrews when 11 clubs participated. George Glennie and John Stewart, representing the Blackheath Club, were victorious. The next year this event was changed to individual match play, and W. Robert Chambers won to become the first amateur champion golfer. George Condie won in 1859.[33]

The first British Open Championship was held at Prestwick in 1860. Eight professionals entered and "Old" Willie Park of Musselburgh was victorious. He played three rounds over the 12-hole course in 174 strokes.[34] The prize was the Championship Challenge Belt, which was donated by the Earl of Eglinton. It had to be won three consecutive times for permanent possession. Actually, the Open Championship sprang from the amateur events held at St. Andrews prior to 1860, and the original concept was a tournament for amateurs only.[35]

"Old" Tom Morris won the second and third

Captain Robert T. Boothby preparing to play. This photograph was taken in the 1850's at the Royal and Ancient Golf Club at St. Andrews, Scotland. Left, standing on walk, is Tom Morris. Allan Robertson, in dark trousers, is on the famed rock bridge which spans the treacherous "Swilcan Burn." (Photo by courtesy of William Blackwood & Sons, Ltd., London, England) Caption from H.S.C. Everard, *A History of the R & A Golf Club,* Wm. Blackwood & Sons, 1897.

Allan Robertson, the famed St. Andrews professional and the "Featherball" champion of the world. Allan was instrumental, in conjunction with Sir Hugh Playfair, in making the Royal and Ancient Golf Club into the leading golf club of the world. Allan was never defeated. His coolness was unique, and almost miraculous. (Photo by courtesy of William Blackwood & Sons Ltd., London, England) Caption from James Linsay Stewart, *Golfiana Miscellanea,* Hamilton, Adams & Co., 1887.

Colonel James O. Fairlie and his caddie, Sand Pirie. Colonel Fairlie was instrumental in forming the Prestwick Golf Club in Ayr, Scotland, in 1851. This club instituted the British Open Championship and was the venue of the British open from 1860 to 1872. (Photo by courtesy of William Blackwood & Sons, Ltd., London, England)

George Glennie putting, and a group of other leading amateurs (gentlemen golfers), and professionals in 1856. George won the Royal Medal of the Royal and Ancient Golf Club with a record 88, which stood for 29 years. (Photo by courtesy of William Blackwood and Sons, Ltd., London, England)

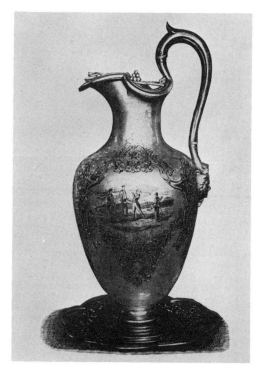

The Silver Claret Jug. The prize of the Golf Club Championship held at St. Andrews in 1857. The Blackheath Golf Club, near London, England, represented by Mr. George Glennie and James Stewart, was victorious. (Photo by courtesy of David Scott Chisholm)

British Opens and Willie Park came back to win the fourth. These two rivals held a monopoly until 1868, when Tom Morris, Jr., the son of "Old" Tom, then only seventeen years of age, won the first of four consecutive titles. Young Tommy became the permanent owner of the Championship Belt in 1870 after winning the Open for the third consecutive time. The championship was cancelled for 1871 and resumed in 1872 when a new championship cup replaced the belt. Young Tommy also won again for his fourth consecutive win.[36]

Tom Morris, Jr., was reputed to be the first immortal professional golfer of the world. His scores broke all previous records and his youthful form executed an excellent follow-through which consti-

FINISH OF THE FIRST AMATEUR GOLF CHAMPIONSHIP
Robert Chambers is seen putting on the last hole at St. Andrews to win the first Amateur Golf Championship in 1858. (Photo by courtesy of William Blackwood and Sons, Ltd., London, England)

WILLIE PARK, SENIOR
Willie Park, the winner of the first British Open Championship in 1860 at the Prestwick Golf Club, Scotland. Willie ultimately won four British Open titles. He was a contemporary of Tom Morris and the two played in many outstanding matches. He represented the Musselburgh Golf Club. (Photo by courtesy of the Neill and Co., Ltd., Edinburgh, Scotland) Caption from Charles Smith, *The Aberdeen Golfers*. Neill & Co., Ltd., 1909.

Tom Morris, the famed professional of the Royal and Ancient
Golf Club of St. Andrews. Tom won a total of four British Open
titles. In 1864 he returned from Prestwick and represented the
Royal and Ancient Golf Club. He became an institution thereat
where he remained until his death in 1908. He played in many
challenge matches with Willie Park. (Photo by courtesy of
David Scott Chisholm) Caption from W. W. Tulloch, *The Life
of Tom Morris*, T. Wernier Laurie, 1907.

The leading professional and amateur of the year in 1862. Tom Morris, left, acting as caddie, successfully defended his British Open title, and James O. Fairlie won three golf club medals including the Royal Medal of the Royal and Ancient G.C., the blue ribbon event for amateur golfers at the time. (Photo by courtesy of William Blackwood and Sons, Ltd., London, England)

Three outstanding amateurs (gentlemen golfers), George Whyte-Melville, Captain Maitland Dougal, and George Glennie.

tuted a complete new swinging form over the old methods.[37] Unfortunately, Young Tom met a tragic death at the youthful age of twenty-four. His death was due to the bursting of an artery in the right lung. He died on Christmas day, 1875. The inscription on his monument reads: "Deeply regretted by numerous friends and all golfers, he thrice won the Championship Belt, and held it without rivalry, and yet without envy, his many amiable qualities being no less acknowledged than his golfing achievements."[38]

The Golfer's Garland

Of rural diversions too long has the Chace
All the honors usurp'd, and assum'd the chief place;
But truth bids the Muse from henceforward proclaim,
That GOFF, first of sports, shall stand foremost in frame.

O'er the Heath, see our heroes in uniform clad,
In parties well match'd, how they gracefully spread;
While with long strokes and short strokes they tend to the
    goal,
And with putt well directed plump into the hole.

At Goff we contend without rancour or spleen,
And bloodless the laurels we reap on the green;
From vig'rous exertions our raptures arise,
And to crown our delights no poor fugitive dies.

From exercise keen, from strength active and bold,
We'll traverse the green, and forget we grow old;
Blue devils, diseases, dull sorrow, and care,
Knock'd down by our balls as they whizz thro' the air.

Health, happiness, harmony, friendship, and fame,
Are the fruits and rewards of our favorite game.
A sport so distinguish'd the fair must approve:
Then to Goff give the day, and the ev'ning to love.

Our first standing toast we'll to Goffing assign,
No other amusement's so truly divine;
It has charms for the aged, as well as the young,
Then as first of field sports let its praises be sung.

The next we shall drink to our friends far and near,
And the memory of those who no longer appear;
Who have play'd their last round, and pass'd over that
    bourne
From which the best Goffer can never return.

(First golf song ever published)[39]

Charlie Hunter, left, and Tom Morris at the Prestwick St. Nicholas Golf Club, Prestwick, Ayrshire, 1863. Tom was the professional at Prestwick at the time but later returned to St. Andrews, his native town. In 1868 Charlie Hunter became the professional at Prestwick and remained for 53 years, until his death in 1921. (Photo by courtesy of the Prestwick Golf Club) Caption from James E. Shaw, *Prestwick Golf Club,* Jackson, Son & Co., 1938.

Tom Morris, Jr., wearing the famous Championship Belt which became his permanent property in 1870 after winning three consecutive British Open titles. Young Tom also won in 1872 for four consecutive wins. (The British Open not played in 1871.) He was only seventeen years old when he won his first title. Young Tom met a tragic death on Christmas day at his youthful age in 1875. He was considered without refute as the first immortal professional golfer of the world. (Photo by courtesy of David Scott Chisholm) Caption from W. W. Tullock, *The Life of Tom Morris,* T. Werner Laurie, 1908.

THE FIRST PICTORIAL EVIDENCE OF GOLF BEING PLAYED IN ENGLAND

Long before Scotland and England wrote about the subject of golf, the Dutch Artists thrived on golf paintings. The golfer depicted above is in the east window of Gloucester Cathedral, England. This window dates from the mid-fourteenth century and is the only pictorial evidence of golf being played in England at the time. (Photo by courtesy of the Dean and Chapter of Gloucester Cathedral)

This most historical page from a Flemish book of Hours was executed between 1500–1520 by Simon Bennink, a renown artist during the time of Queen Katherine. At the foot of the calendar devoted to the month of September is a miniature which by its roughness, compared to Bennink's own work, is suggestively the effort of a pupil. It is the closest resemblance of golf as played in Scotland during this period. Furthermore, it is one of the earliest paintings in Holland which actually depicts golf clubs, balls and a hole. The game is also being played on ground, not ice. This book of Hours, bought from Ernest, Baron de Polnitz of Schloss Babenwohl, Bregenz, on April 13, 1861, and known as *The Golf Book* in the British Museum, consists of thirty vellum folios bound in book form. This miniature has been reproduced in several books on golf, but without stress on a significance that it is surely arresting; i.e., golf in the same, if primitive, form as used today, depicted at the time, the early sixteenth century. (Sir Guy Campbell, *History of Golf in Britain.* Shenval Press, 1952)

A young Dutch (boy) golfer of the seventeenth century. A number of articles have been written about this painting, by Albert Cuyp, (1650), in which they referred this golfer to be a girl, but actually he is a boy. (Photo reproduced from a painting by Albert Cuyp. Courtesy of the Late D. Scot Chisholm)

Mr. John Whyte-Melville, one of the true Christian leaders of
the Royal and Ancient Golf Club. He was captain of the club in
1823 and served in some capacity until 1873. (Photo by courtesy
of William Blackwood & Sons, Ltd., London. From the portrait
painted by R & A G.C., by Sir Francis Grant, P.R.A.)

David Strath, friendly foe and golfing contemporary of Young Tom Morris. The two were the leading professionals in the late 1860's and 1870's. Although David never won the British Open title he was second only to Young Tom. He was runner-up on two occasions. Both these youthful professionals died at an early age, Tom in 1875 and David in 1878. David was the professional at Prestwick Golf Club. (Photo by courtesy of David Scott Chisholm) Caption from Horace G. Hutchinson, *The Badminton Library,* Longmans, Green & Co., 1890.

Mr. John Dun, the captain of the Royal Liverpool Golf Club in 1874. He won the first gold medal of the club in 1870 when it commenced its first championship. It was the Royal Liverpool G.C. which held the first British Amateur Championship in 1885. (Photo by courtesy of the Royal Liverpool Golf Club) Caption from Guy B. Farrar, *The Royal Liverpool Golf Club,* Willmer Bros., & Co., 1933.

Composed for the Blackheath Golf Club, and often sung with great spirit at the celebration of the Ludi Apollinares of Edinburgh. This song must have been written previous to 1783, as it is printed in the Appendix to the third edition of Mathison's poem of "The Goff," published in that year.[40]

In 1864 golf made further progress in England. Apart from the famed Blackheath Golf Club near London, golf was not popular in England until the latter part of the nineteenth century. In 1818 there was a course on Kersal Moor, near Manchester. During this period there were as many golf courses in India as in England, clubs having been formed at Calcutta in 1829 and at Bombay in 1842. Golf was introduced to the continent of Europe in 1814, when two officers from Scotland billeted at Pau after the battle of Orthez and laid out a course which became the Pau Golf Club of France. In 1864 the first English seaside links was laid out at Westward Ho. In the year following, London got its second course when Earl Spencer gave permission for the golfers of the London Scottish Volunteers to construct a course on the Wimbledon Common. In 1869 the Royal Liverpool Golf Club laid out the famous links at Hoylake.[41] The player most responsible for the golf boom in England was Lord Balfour, whose fondness for the game received more than its share of publicity when he was appointed Chief Secretary for Ireland in 1887. At that time the Phoenix Park murders were fresh in everybody's mind and marked the office of the Secretary as one of considerable personal danger. Lord Balfour's visits to the golf links, under the adequate protection of a couple of detectives, were rightly regarded as the strongest possible tribute to the fascination of the game. His personality, moreover, was such as to attract the social world. He was not, however, the pioneer of golf in Ireland. Some period about the time of the Crimean War the officers of the Scottish regiments quartered at the Curragh had started what is now the Royal Curragh Golf Club, and in 1881 the Royal Belfast Club had established itself in its first home at "the Kinnegar." On this side of the Atlantic, Canada, the Royal Montreal Golf Club was formed in 1873, to be followed in 1875 by the Quebec, and in 1876 by the Toronto Club.[42]

"Mrs. Foreman's," the famous inn on the Musselburgh Links, where many Oldtimers have refreshed. The flag on the right is the third green where Tom Morris & Willie Park's big challenge was disrupted and discontinued in 1879 due to the unruly spectators. The Musselburgh course was the home of the Honorable Co., of Edinburgh Golfers, the Oldest Golf Club in the world, during a period. (Photo from the book *Famous Golf Links,* by Horace G. Hutchinson)

Putting on the first green of the Royal and Ancient Golf Club Course in 1883. Tom Morris, standing between the caddies, was the professional at St. Andrews. He is playing with two "gentlemen golfers." The Swilcan burn and the Royal clubhouse is in the background. The clubhouse was completed in 1854 and still stands today. Note one caddy using golf bag which came into existence during the 1880's, while the other is carrying them loosely in arm pit, which was the method used for centuries prior. (Reproduced from a photo in possession of the Royal & Ancient Golf Club) Caption from W. W. Tulloch, *The Life of Tom Morris,* T. Werner Laurie, London 1907.

George Glennie. outstanding amateur golfer and prominent golf leader for many years. He won the Royal Medal in 1855 with a record 88 which stood for 29 years. He was the captain of the Blackheath Golf Club in 1862 and 1863. In 1884 he was the captain of the Royal and Ancient Golf Club. In 1881, both the Blackheath Club and the Royal and Ancient Golf Club commenced a tournament in his honor. (Photo by courtesy of William Blackwood & Sons, Ltd., 1897) Caption from H.S.C. Everard, *A History of the Royal & Ancient G.C.,* Wm. Blackwood & Sons, Ltd., London, England.

Bob Ferguson was the third to win three consecutive British Open titles. He almost won four but lost in a playoff to Willie Fernie in 1883. (Photo by courtesy of the Royal Aberdeen Golf Club) Caption from Charles Smith, *The Aberdeen Golfers,* Neill & Co., Ltd., Edinburgh, 1909.

In 1885 the Royal Liverpool Golf Club instituted an amateur championship which later became the first British Amateur Championship. The winner of this event was not recognized as official until 1922. A. F. MacFie was declared the original winner, defeating Horace G. Hutchinson, later an outstanding golf writer, in the finals. Forty-eight entries were charged one guinea to participate.[43] In the following year, Horace G. Hutchinson won over Henry Lamb at St. Andrews, and in 1887, he won again, this time over John Ball, Jr., at the Liverpool Golf Club.[44]

In the British Open Championship during the same year, Willie Park, Jr., son of "Old" Willie, who had won the first British Open, was victorious at Preswick Golf Club. Willie, Jr., repeated his victory in 1889 at Musselburgh where he defeated Andrew Kirkaldy in a playoff. Andrew Kirkaldy had missed a *one inch putt*, which cost him the championship. He attempted to hole out with one hand. When asked by the marker if he tried to putt that shot, he replied, "Yes, and if the hole was big enough I'd like to bury myself in it."[45]

With golf's rapid progress throughout the British Empire and its ever increasing popularity, it was inevitable that the game should gravitate to the United States. Golf was played in the United States before 1887, but it was not until that year that the first permanent American golf club was organized and which remained in continual existence. As early as 1779, there is evidence that golf was played in the United States near New York. Golf was also played in other states; in Georgia, South Carolina, West Virginia, and Virginia, among others. [46 & 47]

For many years the St. Andrews Golf Club, established in 1888, in New York, was considered as the first permanent golf club in the United States. However, it was just recently discovered that the Foxburg Golf Club, in Foxburg, Pa., has legal claim to this distinction. The records of the Pennsylvania Historical Commission and the Encyclopedia Britannica establishes 1887 as Foxburg's date of origin.[48]

South Carolina Golf Club issued notices in the Charleston *City Gazette* in 1788, and Mr. Rivington, the King's Printer in New York, imported, as a

Archie Simpson, runner-up in the British Open in 1885, is driving. Douglas Rolland, runner-up in the Open of 1884, is looking on in an exhibition match on an inland course in England while a group of "chilly" spectators are looking on. (Photo by courtesy of David Scott Chisholm)

Horace G. Hutchinson, winner of the second and third British Amateur Championships. He was also the runner-up in the very first British Amateur event in 1885. Later, Mr. Hutchinson wrote many books on the subject of golf. His first book in 1891 was followed by a dozen more before 1920. (Photo by courtesy of Walery Publishers, London, England)

A most interesting photograph taken in the late 1880's. John Ernest Laidlay, winner of the British Amateur Championship in 1889, is putting, during a match with Horace G. Hutchinson and John Ball. Note: the caddies carrying the golf clubs in the recently introduced golf bags in a most awkward fashion. For centuries prior to this period, clubs were merely carried loosely in the hands and arms. (Photo by courtesy of D. M. Mathieson, *Golf Monthly*)

side line, "veritable Caledonian balls" in 1799. But the real founder of the great American golfing empire was Mr. John Reid, a Scotsman by birth, at Yonkers, a suburb of New York.[49]

Conceding the validity that the Foxburg Country Club was founded in 1887, the birth of golf in the United States took place in the home of Mr. John Reid. This historic event occurred on Wednesday night, November 14, 1888. Mr. Reid invited three friends to dinner — Henry O. Tallmadge, John B. Upham, Kingman Putnam — and they founded the St. Andrews Club. Reid was elected president, and Upham, secretary and treasurer. The others comprised the Board of Governors. The course was a three-hole layout in Reid's cow pasture. It was then moved to a 30-acre tract where six holes were laid out. The next move was to an apple orchard on Palisade Avenue, at which location these pioneer golfers became known as the "Apple Tree Gang." The club made another move in 1894, to Grey Oaks, where nine holes were laid out. It was to move again in August, 1897, to its present location in Mt. Hope in Westchester County, New York, where the club remains today.[50]

As the St. Andrews Golf Club was moving from one location to another, other infant clubs were making even greater progress. The Chicago Golf Club in Wheaton, Illinois, established an 18-hole course through the efforts of Charles B. Macdonald, the great Western golf pioneer. Shinnecock Hills, which was incorporated in 1891, had a 12-hole course and a clubhouse one year after activation. Another progressive club was the Newport Golf Club in Newport, Rhode Island, which made an indelible mark in the history of American golf when it staged the first amateur championship.[51]

Within a very few years after America's first permanent golf club was established, some 50 new clubs were formed in all parts of the United States, not including Canada, where the first permanent club on this side of the Atlantic was formed in Montreal in 1873.[52]

A list of the early American golf clubs, showing their claimed year of activation, follows:[53]

1887—Foxburg Country Club, Foxburg, Pa.
1888—St. Andrews Golf Club, Yonkers, N. Y.

1889—Tuxedo Golf Club, Tuxedo Park, N. Y.
1890—Newport Golf Club, Newport, R. I.
1890—Middlesboro Golf Club, Middlesboro, Ky.
1890—Hotel Champlain Golf Course, Bluff Pt., N. Y.
1891—Philadelphia Country Club, Philadelphia, Pa.
1891—Shinnecock Hills Golf Club, Southampton, N. Y.
1892—Baltimore Golf Club, Baltimore, Md.
1892—Chicago Golf Club, Wheaton, Ill.
1892—Warren's Farm Golf Club, Boston, Mass.
1892—Powelton Golf Club, Newburgh, N. Y.
1893—The Country Club, Brookline, Mass.
1893—Essex County Country Club, Manchester, Mass.
1893—Swannanoa Golf Club, Asheville, N. C.
1893—Chevy Chase Club, Chevy Chase, Md.
1893—Montclair Golf Club, Montclair, N. J.
1894—Tacoma Golf Club, Tacoma, Wash
1894—Oyster Bay Golf Club, Oyster Bay, N. Y.
1894—Santa Barbara Golf Club, Santa Barbara, Cal.
1894—Meadowbrook Golf Club, Hempstead, N. Y.
1894—Weston Golf Club, Weston, Mass.
1894—Country Club of Lakewood, Lakewood, N. J.
1894—Town and Golf Club, Colorado Springs, Colo.
1894—Norwich Golf Club, Norwich, Conn.
1894—Richmond County Country Club, Staten Island, N. Y.
1894—Baltusrol Golf Club, Springfield, N. J.
1894—Portland Golf Club, Portland, Ore.
1894—Erlington Golf Club, Seattle, Wash.
1894—Albany Country Club, Albany, N. Y.
1894—Fairfield Golf Club, Greenwich, Conn.
1894—Otsego Golf Club, Otsego, N. Y.
1894—Apawamis Golf Club, Rye, N. Y.
1894—New Brunswick Golf Club, New Brunswick, N. J.
1894—Riverside Golf Club, Riverside, Cal.
1894—Jekyll Island Golf Club, Brunswick, Ga.
1894—Morris County Golf Club, Convent, N. J.
1894—Staatsburgh Golf Club, Staatsburgh, N. Y.

This historic picture is the first photograph of golf in America at the St. Andrews Golf Club in Yonkers, New York in 1888. Left to rght are Harry Holbrook, A. Kinman, John B. Upham, and John Reid, founder of the golf club and noted as the "Father of American Golf." (Photo by courtesy of the Bettman Archives, New York)

1894—Knollwood, Golf Club, White Plains, N. Y.

1894—Devon Golf Club, Devon, Pa.

1894—Westbrook Country Club, Great River, N. Y.

1894—Patterson Golf Club, Hohokus, N. J.

Many of the above clubs changed courses and names after activation.

(After many years of research, the above listed clubs were published in the original *Encyclopedia of Golf* in 1958. Although many clubs wrote to claim earier dates of activation, only one was substantiated with written evidence. This does not purport that all are precisely correct.)

The first British Ladies Championship was held on the links of Lytham and St. Annes in 1893. Lady Margaret Scott was the first winner. There were 38 contestants in this first championship. The event was sponsored by the Ladies' Golf Union which had originated during the same year.[54 & 55]

The first Ladies Golf Club was instituted in 1868 at St. Andrews, and during the same year The Westward Ho and the North Devon Ladies' Club were established. Apart from the alleged account of Mary Queen of Scots enjoying the game, the ladies heretofore were not too active. The first official account of ladies golf appeared in the minutes of the Musselburgh Golf Club records in 1810. The minutes quote: "The Club to present by subscription a handsome new creel and shawl to the best female golfer, who plays on the annual occasion."[56]

Lady Margaret Scott also won the second and third British Ladies Championship for three consecutive wins then retired from competitive play. Lady Margaret was reputed without contradiction as the first female immortal golfer. She defeated all competitors by large margins.[57]

In 1895, some 40 more golf courses were formed in the United States. As the game expanded in the United States, it did likewise in other countries. The table below indicates the number of golf courses existing world wide from 1890 through 1895:[58]

YEAR	NUMBER OF GOLF COURSES
1890	387
1891	529
1892	634
1893	759
1894	999
1895	1280

In 1894 the first amateur championship in the United States was sponsored by Theodore Havemeyer, president of the Newport Golf Club. It brought together 20 golfers from other leading clubs and was won by Willie G. Lawrence with a score of 188 over 36 holes. Charles Blair Macdonald followed with a 189. The following month, the St. Andrews Club sponsored a similar tournament in which Laurence W. Stoddart defeated Macdonald

John Ball, Jr., the first amateur golfer of the British Empire to claim the mark of immortality. He won a record of eight British Amateur Championships, his first coming in 1888. In 1890, he won both the British Open and the British Amateur Championships. His father was the owner of the Royal Hotel which was for a time the clubhouse of the Royal Liverpool Golf Club. (Photo by courtesy of the Royal Liverpool Golf Club) Caption from Guy B. Farrar, *History of the Royal Liverpool Golf Club*, 1933.

A group of the contestants who entered the first British Ladies Golf Championship at St. Annes in 1893. Lady Margaret Scott was victorious in this first event and she also won in the two years following. This first event was held at the short course of Lytham at St. Annes and 38 contestants were entered. (Photo by courtesy of Mills & Boon, Ltd., London, England) Caption from Mabel E. Springer, *Golfing Reminiscences*, Mills & Boon, Ltd., 1924.

Henry O. Tallmadge, the first Secretary of the United States Golf Association. He conceived the idea which led to the formation of the United States Golf Association which grew to be the largest golfing fraternity of the world. (Photo by courtesy of the United States Golf Association) Caption from Joseph C. Dey, Jr., *United States Golf Association Journal.*

John Ernest Laidlay, one of the top amateur golfers in the 1880's and 1890's and the winner of the British Amateur Championship of 1889 when he defeated L. B. Melville in the finals at St. Andrews, Scotland. (Photo by courtesy of Crooke Photographers, Edinburgh, Scotland)

Willie Dunn who won the first (unofficial) professional championship in the United States. He defeated Willie Campbell in September of 1894 at Shinnecock Hills Country Club. He scored a 97 to Willie Campbell's 100. This was the first golf match of any significance ever held in the United States. (Photo by courtesy of David Scott Chisholm) Caption from James P. Lee, *Golf in America*, Dodd, Mead & Co., New York, 1895.

Mr. Theodore Havemeyer, first president of the United States
Golf Association and the founder of the Newport Golf Club.
He donated the first U.S.G.A. Championship Cup which was
later destroyed by fire. His administrative ability was combined with the most lovable characteristics of a gentleman
sportsman, and the Association was extraordinarily fortunate
in his selection for its first president. (Photo by courtesy of
Henry O. Havemeyer) Caption from Charles Blair Macdonald,
Scotland's Gift Golf, Charles Scribner's Sons, 1928.

The leaders of the 1894 British Ladies Championship. Left to right: Miss Pearson, runner-up, Miss Starkie, semi-finalist, and the "immortal" Lady Margaret Scott, the winner. Miss Issette Pearson was instrumental in forming the Ladies Golf Union and was for some time the secretary. This Golf Union was formed in 1893 and the idea to organize such a union was conceived at the Wimbledon Club. (Photo by courtesy of Fry and Elliott, England) Caption from May Hezlet, *Ladies Golf*, Hutchinson and Co., London, 1904.

A scene from the historic British Amateur Championship of 1895 at the Royal and Ancient Golf Club of St. Andrews, Scotland. Frederick Tait is looking over his putt, while John Ball, Jr., is standing and facing the clubhouse. These two contestants, plus Harold H. Hilton, became known as the Amateur "Triumvirate." Freddy lost this match and, eventually, Mr. Ball was defeated on the 19th hole by Mr. Leslie Melville. (Photo by courtesy of David Scott Chisholm) Caption from John L. Low, F. G. Tait, *A Record*, J. Nisbet & Co., Ltd., 1900.

Henry O. Havemeyer, son of Theodore, the first president of the United States Golf Association, and Henry R. Winthrop. Photo taken during an early American Golf match. (Photo by Courtesy of Henry O. Havemeyer)

on the 19th hole in match play. Macdonald, who learned his golf from the "old school," at Musselburgh, Scotland, took both defeats bitterly. He protested loud and clear. He advocated that the championships were not properly executed under the rules of golf laid down by the Royal and Ancient Golf Club of St. Andrews. His cries were not in vain. The controversies arising from these two events alerted leading golf officials, and they recognized the need for an organized golf association.[59]

Henry O. Tallmadge invited five leading clubs to send representatives to a dinner in New York for the purpose of establishing a governing body for American golf.

The clubs answered the call, and on December 22, 1894, the Amateur Golf Association of the

Lady Margaret Scott, the first feminine immortal golfer. Lady Margaret won the first three consecutive British Ladies Golf Championships then retired from competitive play. She won in 1893 through 1895. Her excellent style of play was exceeded only by her beauty. Later, she played many friendly matches on the Continent. (Photo by Courtesy of Golfing Annual) Caption from David S. Duncan, *The Golfing Annual*, Horace Cox, 1896.

A panoramic scene of the 1898 British Amateur Championship at the Royal Liverpool Golf Club of Hoylake. Freddy Tait, the eventual winner, is lining up his putt. It was Freddy's second British Amateur victory. In the following year, Lieutenant Tait departed for South Africa and participated in the Boer War. He was killed in action in 1900. (Photo by courtesy of David Scott Chisholm) Caption from John L. Low, F. G. Tait, *A Record*, J. Nisbet & Co., Ltd., 1900.

The great Harry Vardon, who had won three out of the last four British Open Championships from 1896 through 1899, made a good-will tour to the United States in 1900. His trip was commercially sponsored by the Spalding people to promote the "Vardon Flyer" golf ball. During his visit, Vardon participated in approximately 67 golf matches. He won over 50, lost 2, halved 2 and lost 11 while playing against the better ball of two opponents. He also won the U.S. Open Championship. His venture to America had a magnetic impact and it proved a potent stimulant to American golf. (Photo by courtesy of David Scott Chisholm) Caption from Harry Vardon, *My Golfing Life*, McClure, Phillips & Co., 1905.

United States was formed at the Calumet Club. The association later changed its title to the American Golf Association, as it was also connected with professional golf, and then to the United States Golf Association, its present name.[60]

These officials constituted the first executive committee of the association: president, Theodore A. Havemeyer, Newport Golf Club; vice-president, Laurence Curtis, The Country Club; vice-president, Charles B. Macdonald, The Chicago Golf Club; secretary, Henry O. Tallmadge, St. Andrews Golf Club; treasurer, Samuel L. Parrish, Shinnecock Hills Golf Club.[61]

In 1895, the United States Golf Association sponsored its first three annual championships — the Men's Amateur, the Men's Open and the Women's Amateur. The Men's Amateur was held at Newport where Charles B. Macdonald defeated Charles E. Sands in the finals and was awarded a $1,000 cup donated by Theodore Havemeyer, the association's president.[62] The Open Championship followed the next day on the same course where Horace Rawlins was the winner.

The following month, Mrs. Charles B. Brown bested 12 other women to win the first Women's Amateur Championship, over the course at Meadow Brook, in Hempstead, New York.[63]

One of the first projects of the U.S.G.A. was to draw up the rules of the game. John Reid and Charles Macdonald favored the rules of the Royal and Ancient Golf Club and were averse to any changes. The American rules were not changed, with the exception of two which were modified.

2

1900 Through 1930

Shortly after the formation of the U.S. Golf Association a number of sectional golf associations were formed and each held district tournaments within its respective section. Some of the leading associations and the year of institution follow: Metropolitan Golf Association, 1887; Inter-collegiate Golf Association, 1897; Golf Association of Philadelphia, 1897; Western Golf Association, 1899; Pacific Northwest Golf Association, 1899; Southern California Golf Association, 1899; Connecticut Golf Association, 1899.[64]

By 1900, there were over 1,000 golf courses scattered throughout the U.S., and every state, then 48, had at least one course. The U.S. Golf Association, which started with five charter clubs in 1894, had 139 golf club members in March, 1899.[65]

Many professional golfers from Scotland and England came to the U.S. and assisted in golf-course construction programs. Many remained and were awarded with lucrative positions at plush country clubs.[66]

The name of Harry Vardon became prominent in the United States in 1900, during which year the A. G. Spalding Co., sponsored his exhibition tour. Although golf was firmly rooted in the U.S., it was still in its infancy and the exhibition tour of Vardon had a magnetic appeal. At the time Vardon ranked as the greatest golfer of the world. He captured the U.S. Open at the Chicago Club during this venture.[67]

The highlights of the game in 1902 were centered on the innovated rubber ball, which marked the first time in over 50 years that a major change had occurred in the golf ball. Although the rubber ball had been introduced prior to this time, it did not receive international recognition until it was used by the winner of the British Open. "Sandy" Herd's quick conversion from the "gutty" to the rubber ball enabled him to defeat a record number of 111 entries and win the British Open by one stroke over Harry Vardon. Herd's 307 total score was approximately eight strokes lower than the average winning score during the past ten years. Immediately after this championship, the game became completely revolutionized by Dr. Coburn Haskell's rubber ball.[68]

Dr. Haskell conceived the idea for his rubber ball at the Goodrich Rubber Co., in Cleveland. The legality of the Haskell patent was contested on the basis that every substance it comprised had previously been used. However, it was contended that the proportionate arrangement of such elements constituted the invention. At any case, the ball was invented, used, and approved for play; and the only disadvantage it created was the necessity to change certain golf holes to compensate for the additional yardage the ball provided.[69]

The rubber ball also proved its success to Lawrence Auchterlonie in the U.S. Open Championship.

Harold H. Hilton, driving in the finals of the 1901 British Amateur championship at the Royal and Ancient Golf Club of St. Andrews. His opponent, John L. Low, whom he defeated, looks on. Old Tom Morris, the veteran professional, is in his customary position at the tee. Hilton was the defending champion and thus made it two consecutive wins. He later won two more for a total of four titles. (Photo by courtesy of the Royal Liverpool Golf Club) Caption from Guy B. Farrar, *The Royal Liverpool Golf Club*, Wilmer Bros., 1933.

He became the first to break 80 in each of the four rounds to win by six strokes.

Walter J. Travis, better known as the "old man," painted a most unusual picture in the chapters of early American golf. He won the U.S. Amateur three times and the British Amateur in his first and only attempt, in 1904.

During this period the competition of the British Amateur was obviously far superior to the U.S. Amateur, and naturally an American had little or no chance to win. Such were the conditions and circumstances when Travis, with his mallet-head putter and his long black cigars, won the British Amateur.

"Ted" Blackwell was the longest hitter in the game, and Walter J., was one of the shortest on both sides of the Atlantic. The tension of this final match grew tremendously as the two contestants met. Travis was given little or no chance to win. In fact, the British considered him lucky to have reached the title round.

Travis lived up to his reputation as a great putter on the second hole where he canned a 35-foot putt for a winning three to go two up. On the next hole, the "old man" made a complimentary remark to Blackwell about his long drives, but Ted's response was sort of a grunt, and not one word was spoken between the two contestants. The match ended on the 33rd hole when the "old man" sank his final winning putt. There was no applause from the spectators.[70]

Travis never attempted to defend his British Amateur crown nor did he ever enter the championship again. He ended his tournament career in 1915,

Alex 'Sandy' Herd, winner of the British Open Championship in 1902. While the 'Triumvirate' and his other opponents were using the old 'Gutty' ball, Sandy switched to the new innovated rubber ball which contributed to his victory. (Photo by courtesy of Robert E. Harlow, *Golf World* Magazine) Caption from Sandy Herd, *My Golfing Life*, Chapman & Hall, Ltd., 1923.

The first professional international match between Scotland and England in 1903. Harry Vardon, representing England, is seen lining up his putt. (Photo by courtesy of David Scott Chisholm)

Walter J. Travis, reputed to be the first American amateur golfer to reach the mark of immortality. In 1904, he became the first "outsider" to win the British Amateur Championship in one of the most historic events of the world. He was Australian by birth and made America his home. He was one of the greatest putters of all times. (Photo by courtesy of Robert E. Harlow, *Golf World* Magazine)

The honorable Osmund Scott, who at the age of fifty-four, was the runner-up in the British Amateur Championship of 1905. He lost in the finals by three and two to A. G. Barry at Prestwick. Walter J. Travis, who had won the previous year, was referred to as the "old man." Walter was just over forty-two years of age when he won. However, he did not attempt to defend his title. (Photo by courtesy of David Scott Chisholm)

Alex Smith, one of five brothers, all fine professional golfers who migrated to America from the famed Carnoustie in Scotland, won the U.S. Open Championship in 1906 with a record score of 295. Alex repeated in 1910 when he won in a three-way playoff against his brother Macdonald, and Johnny Mc-Dermott. His brother Willie won the U.S. Open in 1899. Alex was a runner-up on two previous occasions in the U.S. Open — once in 1898 and again in 1901. In the latter event, he lost in a playoff to Willie Anderson. In the 1910 Open event, Alex missed a two-foot putt on the last green, 72nd hole, but he came back to win the playoff. (Photo by courtesy of Davd Scott Chisholm)

54

A fine study of "Old" Tom Morris who was an institution at
St. Andrews for many years. He won the British Open four
times when the prize was for the Champonship Challenge
Belt. This shot was taken of the grand old man in front of
his St. Andrews golf shop, prior to his death in 1908. (Photo
by courtesy of David Scott Chisholm)

Miss Dorothy Campbell became internationally famous in 1909 when she became the first to win both the British Ladies Amateur Championship and the United States Womens Amateur Championship during the same year. In the following year, she successfully defended her U.S. Womens Amateur title. Within a three-year period, she won two U.S. Womens Amateur titles, two British Ladies Amateur titles and three Canadian Womens Amateur titles. In 1924, fifteen years after her first U.S. Women's Amateur victory, she was victorious again in the same event. (Photo by courtesy of David Scott Chisholm)

Miss E. Grant Suttie, British Ladies Amateur Champion of 1910, is seen here driving off the first tee of the Royal and Ancient Golf Club of St. Andrews. She won her title at Westward Ho.

winning the Metropolitan Amateur Championship for his fourth time at age fifty-four. His other contributions to the game were in the field of writing. He instituted the *American Golfer* and was the editor for some time. He died in 1927.[71]

The year following Travis' British Amateur victory, professional golf took the limelight. In 1905, Willie Anderson became the first and only golfer to win three consecutive U.S. Open Championships, which gave him a total of four Open titles.

During this era, in Great Britain, the famous three professionals — Harry Vardon, John H. Taylor, and James Braid — became known as "the great triumvirate" and were winning them all. A French professional, Arnaud Massey, took the title away in 1907 for the first time. However, when the trophy returned, it remained in the custody of the "triumvirate" for many years to come.[72]

British subjects were still winning the U.S. Open title until 1911. That year John J. McDermott of the Atlantic City Country Club became the first homebred to win. Young Johnny was only 19 when

he defeated another native son Mike Brady in a playoff at the Chicago G. C., in Wheaton, Ill., to win. He successfully defended his title during the following year at the Country Club of Buffalo.[73]

It was in the following year, September, 1913, that a youthful amateur, twenty-year-old Francis Ouimet, achieved one of the most dramatic victories the golf world has ever known. It happened near Boston, at the Country Club, Brookline, Mass., where a record number of 165 contestants were vying for the nation's most coveted trophy, the U.S. Open Championship. Among the participants was Harry Vardon, the immortal British golfer and undisputed world's greatest. Another great golfer on hand was Edward "Ted" Ray, the 1912 British Open king and the longest hitter in the game.

At the end of 36 holes, Vardon was leading, with another British professional, Wilfred Reid, at 147, two strokes ahead of Ted Ray. At the end of 54 holes Vardon was tied for the lead with Ray and an unknown amateur, Francis Ouimet, at 225. Ouimet, who had shot a 74 on the third round, was unknown

James Braid, the tallest member of the famed "triumvirate," became the first golfer to win five British Open Championships, which he succeeded in doing in 1910 at St. Andrews, Scotland. (Photo by courtesy of David Scott Chisholm)

Fred Herreshoff, the runner-up in the 1911 U.S. National Amateur Championship. Freddy strived in vain to prevent the trophy from leaving the U.S., but he was defeated on the 37th hole by Harold H. Hilton, an immortal British Amateur. Thus the U.S. Amateur trophy departed the United States for the first time. (Photo by courtesy of David Scott Chisholm)

John Ball, Jr., the first British immortal amateur golfer. In 1912, John won his *seventh* British Amateur Championship when he defeated Abe Mitchell on the 38th hole at Westward Ho. It is a record which has never been approached. Twenty-two years ago, he won his first Amateur Championship. In 1890, he won both the British Open and Amateur Championships in the same year. (Photo by courtesy of Robert E. Harlow, *Golf World* Magazine)

Edward "Ted" Ray wedged out the "triumvirate" in 1912 and won the British Open Championship by four strokes at Muirfield, Scotland. During this period, Big Ted was the longest hitter in the game, and he always drew a large gallery, regardless of his play. (Photo by courtesy of David Scott Chisholm)

John H. Taylor, "the shortest" of the "triumvirate," became the third golfer to win five British Open Championships which he succeeded in doing in 1913 at the Royal Liverpool Golf Club. His 304 total score was eight strokes in front of Edward "Ted" Ray, who came in second. (Photo by courtesy of David Scott Chisholm)

outside of Massachusetts, and it was presumed that he would never hold his own in the fourth and last round. Ray came in with a 72-hole total of 304. So far, it was the leading score. Ray sat by and smoked his familiar pipe and waited for the others to arrive. One by one they came in and the score stood up. Then Vardon came in with the same score and Ray's biggest worries were over. Ouimet had taken a 43 on the first nine and started with a five on the short tenth. It appeared a certainty that the two favorites, Vardon and Ray, would vie in a playoff. Word was then passed around that Ouimet had a very slim chance of tieing. He was informed on the 13th tee that he needed to play the remaining six holes in two

under par in order to tie, a most improbable feat over the wet Brookline course. But with the aid of his ten-year-old caddie, Ouimet birdied the 13th with a chip shot and sank a 20-foot putt on the 17th. He now had to par the 18th. By this time the gallery was wild. On the 18th he hit a fair drive and was slightly short with his approach. His chip shot was about four feet short. He putted without hesitation, and the ball found the hole. The crowd went wild with excitement; he had tied the great Vardon and Ray for the title.[74]

Little chance was given the young amateur to win the playoff, but with the aid of his same ten-year-old caddie, Eddie Lowery, Ouimet stepped to

Harold H. Hilton was the second British amateur golfer to reach the height of immortality. By 1913, he had won four British Amateur titles, two British Open titles, four Irish Open titles and one United States Amateur Championship. Not only a master golfer but an excellent golf writer. He wrote five outstanding books and was the first editor of *Golf Monthly*, the best golf magazine of Great Britain. (Photo by courtesy of Robert E. Harlow, Golf World Magazine)

"THE TRIUMVIRATE"

The famed "Trio" who practically dominated the British Golf titles from 1894 to 1914: Harry Vardon driving, James Braid standing, and John H. Taylor sitting. The three won 16 British Open titles and countless other tournaments during this period. (Photo by Robert E. Harlow, *Golf World* Magazine) (From an Oil painting by Clement Flower)

Francis Ouimet and his ten-year old caddy, Eddie Lowery, at the Country Club, Brookline, Mass., in 1913 when he won the most outstanding playoff in the history of the U.S. Open Championship. He defeated the immortal Harry Vardon and Edward "Ted" Ray over the soggy Brookline course which stands out as the most dramatic golf victory in the world. First, it marked the first time an amateur had won the U.S. Open Championship. Second, an unknown amateur, outside the state of Mass., defeated the greatest golfer in the world, Harry Vardon. And he did it in the most difficult and unexpected method, in a playoff. He also defeated, in the same media, the longest hitter and the year's previous winner of the British Open Championship, Edward "Ted" Ray. His great victory was a tremendous boost to golf as it stimulated keen interest among all amateur golfers on both sides of the Atlantic. (Photo by courtesy of Francis Ouimet, *A Game of Golf*, Underwood & Underwood, 1933.)

the first tee, having drawn the honors. It was raining over the already wet course. Lowery handed Ouimet the driver and told him, "Be sure and keep your eye on the ball."[75] Ouimet did keep his eye on the ball. He scored a 72. Vardon and Ray took a 77 and 78 respectively. Ouimet's victory became known as the most sensational in the history of golf.[76]

The following year, Ouimet proved his U.S. Open victory was no fluke. He defeated Jerome D. Travers in the final round, to win his second major title, the United States Amateur. Seventeen years later, 1931, Ouimet won this title again.

The year 1914 marked the first major victory of America's Walter Hagen and the last major victory of the famous British "Triumvirate." World War I inflicted its toll on British golf three years before it was to damage golf in the U.S. Thus, the 1914 British Open was the last in which Vardon, Taylor, and Braid played a major role. Up to this event,

each had won five British Open Championships. Which of the trio would be the first and only to win six? This was the question foremost on the minds of 9,000 spectators who added drama to this most spectacular event. It was the 54th British Open, held at Prestwick, where the first one was held in 1860. At the end of the first round, Vardon led with a 73, with Taylor and Braid trailing with 74's. Vardon increased his lead in the second with a 77 while Taylor had a 78 and Braid fell behind with an 82. In the third round, Taylor came through with a 74 which caught and passed Vardon, who scored a 78. Therefore, Taylor was in a commanding position at the end of round three. In the final and decisive round, Taylor increased his lead to three strokes, but at the third (Cardinal) hole, Vardon gained a stroke. Then, at the fourth, Taylor caught the treacherous burn and finally took a seven to Vardon's four, which put Vardon in the lead again. This was Taylor's Waterloo as he was never in seri-

Miss Cecil Leitch, winner of the British Ladies' Championship in 1914. She was later to become one of the greatest lady golfers of the world. (Photo by courtesy of the *American Golfer* Magazine)

Walter C. Hagen, at the age of twenty-two, won the U.S. National Open Championship in 1914 at the Midlothian C.C., Blue Island, Illinois. His name was to reappear again and again in the years to come. (Photo by courtesy of *Golfers* Magazine, by Pietzckes)

Mr. John Taylor
Captain of the Honorable Company of Edinburgh Golfers,
1807, 1808, 1814, 1815, 1823, 1824, and 1825. Mr. Taylor
captained the oldest golf club in the world. He was one of the
finest golfers of his day. (From a portrait by John W. Gordon
1790 - 1864 in possession of the Hon. Co.)

Mr. William Innes, Captain of the Royal Blackheath Golf
Club, England, 1778. The red coat was the uniform for the
Blackheath golfers of the day. The Blackheath Golf Club
was the first golf club in England. Golf was played there in
1608, however, the club was not formed until sometime
later. (Photo by courtesy of the Royal Blackheath Golf Club)
(A print from a lost painting by Lemuel Francis Abbott, RA)

Harry Vardon, the immortal British Professional golfer, reputed without refute to be the greatest golfer of the world,
won his *sixth* British Open crown in 1914. He was the
supreme stylist and no player ever equalled his skill. Of placid
and serene disposition he endeared himself wherever he
played. (Photo by courtesy of David Scott Chisholm)

Part of the gallery at the U.S. Open Championship in 1915 at Baltusrol where Jerome Travers, seen putting, became the second amateur to win the championship. He scored 297 to shade Tom McNamara by one stroke. (Photo by courtesy of David Scott Chisholm)

ous contention again.[77] From here on Vardon took over and won by three strokes. This tournament ended the reign of the famous trio, who had won 16 of the last 20 British Open Championships. This tournament, the granddaddy of them all, was discontinued for six years during the war.[78]

In 1915, Jerome D. Travers became the second amateur to win the U.S. National Open title. It was just one year later that another amateur, Charles "Chick" Evans, of Chicago, won both the U.S. Open Championship and the U.S. National Amateur Championship during the same year. In the Open event, Chick established a record low of 286 which was to stand for 20 years. He used seven "hickory" shafted clubs.[79]

The year 1916 also saw the formation of the Professional Golfers Association of America. The P.G.A. staged its first national championship at Siwanoy Country Club in New York, where James M. Barnes defeated Jock Hutchison in the finals to become the first winner. In 1917 and 1918, this championship was discontinued due to the war. When it was resumed in 1919, James M. Barnes successfully defended his title.

By 1920, the membership of the U.S.G.A. had increased to 477 golf clubs, of which 159 were active and 310 were allied. Chick Evans defeated Francis Ouimet in the final round to win his second U.S. Amateur Championship. The U.S. Open Championship saw Britain's Harry Vardon and Ted Ray regain the limelight. Although British golf had been practically dormant during the previous six

Charles "Chick" Evans of Chicago in 1916 became the first to win the "Double Crown" — the U.S. Open and the U.S. Amateur Championships. With the use of seven hickory-shafted golf clubs, Evans established a record of 286 in winning the U.S. Open title which was to stand for 20 years. During Chick's brilliant golfing career, he won eight Western Amateur titles, two U.S. Amateur Championships, one U.S. Open Championship, and one Western Open title. Later, Chick Evans was instrumental in the activities of the Western Golf Association. Among other things a Caddy Foundation was established in Chick's honor, which provides scholarships for worthy caddies. This association has been extremely successful and has provided hundreds of caddies with funds to obtain a college education. (Photo by courtesy of David Scott Chisholm)

A close-up of the swing of Jerome Dunstan Travers. Between 1906 and 1915, Travers collected five major and five semi-major championships. Included were four U.S. Amateur titles. In his greatest victory, the U.S. Open Championship, he had to play the rough back nine at Baltusrol in one under par in order to win. This he accomplished in spite of hitting one out of bounds on the tenth hole. (Photo by Courtesy of Gene Sarazen. *Thirty Years of Championship Golf*, Prentice Hall, 1950) Caption from Nevin H. Gibson, *The Encyclopedia Of Golf*, A. S. Barnes & Co., 1958.

The honorable Charles E. Hughes, Chief Justice for the U.S. Supreme Court, on the tee at Estes Park, Colorado, in 1916, during vacation. (Photo by courtesy of the *American Golfer* Magazine)

Robert Tyre Jones, Jr., *"Bobby Jones,"* who won the Georgia State Amateur Championship in 1916. His name was to be mentioned again. (Photo by courtesy of the *American Golfer* Magazine, 1916)

James M. Barnes won the first National Professional Golfers Championship in 1916 at the Siwanoy C. C., N. Y. He successfully defended this title in 1919, when the event was resumed after the war. Later, Barnes won the U.S. Open and the British Open Championships. (Photo by courtesy of David Scott Chisholm)

George Duncan once wrote a book entitled *Golf at A Gallop*. It was rightly named about himself as he is the fastest professional champion of all time. This spirited Scot won the British Open Championship in 1920 without half of his followers knowing it — so quickly did he make his shots. One of the most brilliant minds in his profession. (Photo by courtesy of David Scott Chisholm)

Alexander "Sandy" Herd, the first winner of the British Open with rubber "Haskell" golf ball in 1902, was the runner-up in the same event 18 years later in 1920. At this period, Sandy holds the world's record for the number of aces, holes in one' made. He had 19, all authenticated. (Photo by courtesy of David Scott Chisholm)

Miss Alexa Sterling won her third consecutive U.S. Women's Amateur Championship in 1920. Her third victory came at Cleveland where she defeated the immortal Dorothy Campbell (Hurd) in the finals. (Photo by courtesy of Miss Cecil Leitch)

Cecil Leitch, the immortal feminine golfer from across the Atlantic. Cecil won her first British Ladies Amateur Championship in 1914 after which all championships were cancelled due to the war. When resumed in 1920 she won again, and the following year, she successfully defended her title, which gave her three consecutive victories. In 1926 she was to win again for a total of four championship titles. On two occasions, she was a runner-up to Joyce Wethered, who also entered the portal of immortality in later years. (Photo by courtesy of David Scott Chisholm)

Four great amateurs of the world: Bobby Jones, yet to capture a major event; Cyril Tolley, British Amateur king of 1920; Roger Wethered, brother of Joyce, runner-up in the British Open after losing in playoff of 1921; and Francis Ouimet, the U.S. Open winner of 1913 and the U.S. Amateur winner of 1914. (Photo by courtesy of David Scott Chisholm)

Miss Marion Hollins, winner of the U.S. Women's Amateur Championship in 1921 at Deal, N. J., where she defeated Alexa Stirling in the finals and therefore prevented Alexa from winning an unprecedented four straight titles. (Photo by courtesy of Cecil Leitch)

Miss Joyce Wethered, left, congratulates Cecil Leitch, her conqueror, in the final round of the British Ladies' Amateur Championship at Turnberry in 1921. It was the third consecutive title for Miss Leitch. (Photo by courtesy of Cecil Leitch)

years, these two aging notables proved their superiority over the American professionals, with Ray winning and Vardon tying for second. It was to be the last successful British invasion of the U.S. Open.[80]

The first international amateur matches between the United States and Great Britain were held in 1921 at Hoylake, England, with the Americans victorious. These matches were designated the following year as the official Walker Cup Matches in honor of George Herbert Walker, donor of the cup and the outgoing president of the U.S.G.A.[81]

In 1922 the U.S.G.A., under the persuasion of James D. Standish, Jr., inaugurated the Amateur Public Links Championship. The first championship was held in Toledo, Ohio, and Edmund R. Held was the victor.[82]

A former caddie, twenty years of age, Gene Sarazen, rose to the heights of golf glory this same year by winning both the U.S. Open and National P.G.A. Championships. To add further glory, he defeated Walter Hagen in a 72-hole match for the unofficial world's championship.[83]

On the feminine side and on British soil, Joyce Wethered defeated Cecil Leitch to win the British Ladies Championship. Miss Leitch defended her title against the advice of a physician who had treated her for a torn arm muscle. However, she was after her *fourth consecutive* title and could not resist the temptation to try to become the first and only woman to do it.[84]

In 1923, Bobby Jones, the youthful amateur from Atlanta, finally won his first major championship when he defeated Bobby Cruickshank in a playoff for the U.S. Open. It was to be Bobby's first of 13 major championships, a record which has yet to be duplicated. His first victory, after so many failures, is best described by Jones himself. "We were all even on the last and decisive hole. I sliced to the short rough and the ball lay on the hard ground, clean — I suppose I had to decide again whether to play safe or go for it with an iron of about 200 yards. But I don't remember it. Stewart Maiden was near me. He told me later that I never played a shot more promptly or decisively. He says I picked a No. two iron from the bag and banged it — I saw the ball on the green near the pin. Next thing I knew somebody was propping me up by the arm — I won the hole with a four to Bobby's six. And the Championship."[85]

The first international professional matches between the U.S. and Great Britain in 1926 in England, where the British won 13½ to 1½. "Wild" Bill Melhorn scored the only single point for the American team. The following year these matches were played in Massachusetts as the Ryder Cup Matches in honor of Samuel A. Ryder, a wealthy British seed merchant who donated a solid golf trophy. In this event the American team was victorious.[86]

Also in 1926, Bobby Jones became the first to win both the U.S. Open and the British Open in the same year, while Walter Hagen successfully defended the PGA title for his third consecutive win. (The next year he made it four in a row.) These victories earned them the recognition as the greatest amateur and professional in the world. When they met in a memorable 72-hole challenge match in Florida, Hagen was an easy winner by 11 and 10. The first 36 holes were played at St. Petersburg, where Hagen was paid $5,000, and the remaining holes were played at Sarasota Bay, where he received the gate

Prior to the battle for the U.S. Open Championship in 1922 at Skokie C. C., Chicago, Illinois. James M. Barnes, left, was the defending champion for the U.S. trophy, table center, and Walter Hagen, right, had just won the British Open trophy, also seen on the table. However, it was Gene Sarazen who finished victorious with a record-tying 68 to overcome a five-stroke deficit. Hagen, who opened with a 68, finished with a 291 for fifth palce while Barnes fell far below with a 306. It was the first time a gate fee was charged to the spectators. (Photo by courtesy of David Scott Chisholm)

Walter Hagen and Gene Sarazen on the first tee of the Pelham
C. C., N. Y., before their historic 1923 battle for the P.G.A.
Championship. Young Gene defeated King Walter on the 38th
hole. It was the first final decided by extra holes. (Photo by
courtesy of Gene Sarazen) *Thirty Years of Championship
Golf*, Prentice Hall, 1950.

A priceless scene on the 18th hole at Inwood C. C., in 1923
where Robert T. Jones, Jr., won his first major championship after defeating "Wee" Bobby Cruikshank in a playoff.
The famed lagoon, which Bobby cleared with a mid iron on
his second shot, can be seen at the left of the green. The entry
of 360 set a record and qualifying at the scene of the championship required four days. Since the championship proper
took two more days and the playoff another day, a full week
was required to determine the Champion. (Photo by courtesy
of David Scott Chisholm) Caption from *Record Book of the
U.S.G.A. Championships*, 1895 through 1953.

money of $3,500. His $8,500 total was the largest
amount ever received for a single challenge match.
Afterwards, the U.S.G.A. banned amateurs from
playing in such events.[87]

American golf during the roaring twenties, the
golden decade of sports, was the most spectacular
in the history of the game. Hagen and Jones were
the idols of the golfing world and contributed im-
measurably to the great popularity the game at-
tained.[88]

In 1927 Walter Hagen won his fourth consecutive
National P.G.A. Championship which gave him a
total of five. This record remains the greatest match
play achievement in the history of golf. During this
same year "The Haig" also won his fourth Western
Open Championship which was also a record num-

ber of wins. He was to win his fifth in 1932.[89] During this period, Walter Hagen and Bobby Jones
were the idols of the golfing world. Before the end
of Sport's Golden Decade, 1920 through 1930,
Jones won 13 major championships and Hagen won
11. These records have yet to be duplicated.

Many writers have described the great triumphs
of the "fabulous Haig" during the bygone years. The
late Grantland Rice described him most superbly
just before he departed for greener fairways. Granny
quotes: "Walter Hagen, a dazzling ornament to the
history of sport, had the soundest golf philosophy
I've ever known. More important, he applied it."
"All told, Hagen won 11 National and International
crowns — second only to Bobby Jones." "Walter
Hagen didn't change the social system of the British

Jack Jolly, left, professional golfer and one of the greatest authorities on early professional golf in the United States; and Jack Burke, Sr., father of Jack Burke, Jr., in 1923 at the Inwood C. C., N. Y., during the U.S. Open. (Photo by courtesy of David Scott Chisholm)

The "Haig's" great popularity in Great Britain is vividly revealed by the smiling expressions of the presenting officials of the Royal Liverpool Golf Club of England in 1924. It was Walter's second of four British Open victories. (Photo by courtesy of Bertram Eary, Great Britain)

Miss Joyce Wethered with the British Ladies' Championship trophy she won at Troon in 1925 after defeating the immortal Cecil Leitch in the finals on the 37th hole. Miss Wethered was the defending champion. (Photo by courtesy of the Central Press Photos Ltd., London, England)

Two very great golfers in serious conference: John H. Taylor, left, who won five British Open Championships of England and Macdonald Smith who was universally hailed as the outstanding professional who never won a major championship. Macdonald Smith possessed one of the most beautiful swings in golf. (Photo by courtesy of David Scott Chisholm)

Miss Glenna Collett participating in the British Ladies' Amateur Championship in 1925 at Troon. This was one event which Glenna could never capture although she was later a runner-up on two occasions. She was to win a total of six U.S. Women's Amateur Championships, for a record which has never been approached. (Photo by courtesy of Miss Cecil Leitch)

Plus fours (baggy knickers) were quite popular during the twenties as evidenced by this photo taken in 1925 at the Rancho Golf Club in Los Angeles. Here we see, from left to right, Tommy Armour, George Von Elm, Bobby Cruikshank, Jackie Coogan of moving picture fame, and Scotty Armstrong. (Photo by courtesy of David Scott Chisholm)

Two friendly rivals, Leo Diegel and Walter Hagen, in 1926
at Long Beach, California. These two fought many National
P.G.A. battles down to the wire. In 1926, the "Haig" defeated
Leo in the finals for his three consecutive victories. In the
following year, he repeated for his fourth consecutive championship — a record which has never been approached.
(Photo by courtesy of David Scott Chisholm)

Isles, but his easy grace and deportment helped
soften it somewhat. Hagen had an eye for style and
plush. He liked to be driven from his hotel to the
first tee by a liveried chauffeur, preferably in a Rolls
Royce." "He was golf's greatest showman. He
'staged' many shots that looked hard but were not.
But he could make hard ones with the easier
chances." "I can't tell you how many times I've seen
Hagen arrive at the club house only ten minutes
before starting time, still in his night-club uniform,
dinner jacket and all. He'd saunter through his
change, knock over a scotch and turn in a 70 without batting an eye." "Hagen was the first golfer to
make a million dollars — and the first to blow it!

I recall when he made a world tour — Japan, Australia, India — all over the map. He had 5,000
dollars on his person, or within quick reach, when
he left. He won 14,000 dollars in several big tournaments. But when he returned to the old U.S.A.,
he had to borrow a dollar from his manager, Bob
Harlow, to pay his taxi fare. Money — a dollar or
10,000 — meant nothing to Hagen." "But this I'll
say for Hagen. He had won five PGA matches going
into that final in the 1923 PGA. He then proceeded
to win in 1924, 1925, 1926, and 1927, and he went
to the final round in 1928. That means that Hagen
won 34 of 36 matches from the greatest golfers in
the world — 29 of those matches in succession. It

Dashing "Light-Horse" Harry Cooper lost in a playoff against Tommy Armour, the Silver Scot, in the U.S. Open Championship in 1927 at the Oakmont (Pa) Country Club. Harry had three putted the lightning fast green in the championship proper and Tommy sank a ten-foot birdie putt for the tie, then won the playoff. (Photo by courtesy of David Scott Chisholm)

Just before the battle for the U.S. Amateur Championship in
1927 at Minneapolis. Bobby Jones was defeated by George
Von Elm the previous year which prevented Jones from winning three straight titles. However, Jones was not to be
denied in this event. He defeated "Chick" Evans in the finals
by 8 and 7, while Von Elm lost in the first round to Harry G.
Legg, the Western Amateur champion of 1919. A very famous
photo and highly praised by both champions. (Photo by
Courtesy of David Scott Chisholm)

One of the very greatest pictures ever taken of Bobby Jones. It illustrates a most vivid expression of determination, concentration, and a fighting spirit which are the qualities possessed by this immortal amateur. Taken at Minneapolis in 1927 when Bobby was playing against "Chick" Evans in the U.S. Amateur event. (Photo by courtesy of David Scott Chisholm)

was one of the finest chapters in golf's long history, an incredible performance. Hagen was the match-play king, and that goes for all time. He had no equal when it was man-to-man." "Hagen was a great putter. But Hagen's following will remember him much longer for his color, his sparkling wit, his impeccable dress, his manners and charm under all conditions, than they will for his putting." "As long as I've known Walter Hagen — 40 years — I've found him without inhibitions of any sort. Whether

he's with the king of England or a broken-down caddie, Hagen has never changed his manner to suit the occasion." "Don't worry — don't hurry. You're here on a short visit. Be sure to smell the flowers." This is *Walter Hagen* as quoted by one of the greatest and most respected sports writers of all time.[90]

Even Henry Cotton, the great British professional, writes of Hagen: "I saw Hagen's hotel bill being paid one day by Bob Harlow from a suitcase full of dollars bills. They had been on an exhibition tour

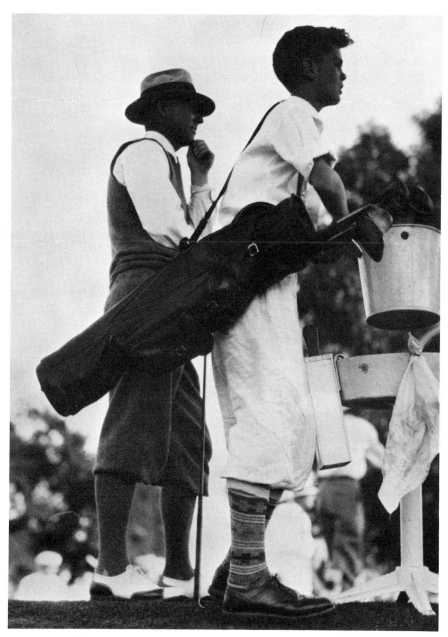

Charles "Chick" Evans, one of the very best amateurs of all times. In 1916 he won both the U.S. Open and the U.S. Amateur in the same year. He won the U.S. Amateur again in 1920. Chick practically dominated the Western Amateur Championship. He won a record eight titles from 1909 through 1923, including four consecutive championships. His name shall forever be boldly emblazoned on the pages of golfing lore. This shot was taken in 1927 at Minneapolis where he lost in the finals of the U.S. Amateur to Bobby Jones. Note Chick's clubs, apart from the putter. They are the same seven hickory-shafted clubs he used in 1916 to establish his great record. Also note the familiar tee maker and ball wash which were quite common during this period. (Photo by courtesy of David Scott Chisholm)

The fabulous Walter Hagen follows through with an iron shot from the tee of a three par hole. He won his fourth consecutive National P.G.A. Championship in 1927 at Dallas, Texas, where he defeated Joe Turnesa in the final round. It was his fifth P.G.A. title, a record never approached. Hagen was no doubt the greatest match player of all time. (Photo by courtesy of David Scott Chisholm)

Tommy D. Armour, "The Silver Scot," won both the U.S. Open and the Canadian Open Championships in 1927. Tommy came to the U.S. from Scotland and played on the first unofficial Walker Cup team for Great Britain and his visit hereto enticed him to remain. (Photo by courtesy of David Scott Chisholm)

These two immortal amateurs made an indelible mark on the history of golf. Bobby Jones, left, was to win the great "Grand Slam" later in 1930, while Francis Ouimet made his biggest mark in 1913 by winning the U.S. Open Championship in the greatest and most dramatic victory the world has ever known. Photo taken in 1927 at Minneapolis. (Photo by courtesy of David Scott Chisholm)

An outstanding threesome: Johnny Farrell, left, the winner of the U.S. Open Championship at Olympia Fields C. C., Illinois, in 1928; George Von Elm, oustanding amateur, who tied with Walter Hagen for fourth place; and Tommy Armour, the Silver Scot, and the defending champion who finished seven strokes back at 301. Farrell won after a playoff against Bobby Jones and the distance was extended to 36 holes, over which Farrell outscored Jones by a single stroke, 143 to 144. (Photo by courtesy of David Scott Chisholm)

An International foursome — Chief Soldani (Indian) Babe
Ruth (Real American and the king of "Swat"), David Scott
Chisholm (Scotch), and Duke Kahanamoku (Hawaiian) —
after a round in Los Angeles. (Photo by courtesy of David
Scott Chisholm)

A picture of the famed Prestwick Golf Club of Scotland, the venue for the 1928 British Amateur Championship and the scene of the first British Open Championship in 1860. Note the railway ties used to keep the drifting sand in place. (Photo by courtesy of David Scott Chisholm)

Characteristic finish of the fabulous Walter C. Hagen who in 1929 won his fourth British Open Championship over the links of Muirfield, Scotland, when he finished six strokes in front of Johnny Farrell, the U.S. Open Champion of 1928. This title gave "The Haig" a total of 11 *major* victories, which is a record in the professional ranks. Bobby Jones, an amateur, who won the "Grand Slam" in the following year, won 13 *major* titles. (Photo by courtesy of David Scott Chisholm)

Diminutive Freddy McLeod, the smallest 108 pounds to win the U.S. Open Championship, back in 1908. Seen here in Los Angeles in 1929, making a swing through the "grapefruit" circuit. Freddy also won the North and South Open in 1920, was the runner-up in the National P.G.A. Championship in 1919 and also the runner-up in the U.S. Open in 1921. (Photo by courtesy of David Scott Chisholm)

Jack Dempsey, World's Heavyweight Champion, tries his hand on the putting green at Los Angeles, Cal., as a guest of the golf writers. Left to right are Bob Edgren, C. Van Dyke, David Scott Chisholm, Darsie L. Darsie, and George O'Neill, all famous in their various fields of endeavor. (Photo by courtesy of David Scott Chisholm)

and collected one dollar at the gate." "Anyone who can arrive two hours late for an exhibition in the midst of a fuming crowd — then say "HOWDY FOLKS" with a big smile, then receive an applause, must have something."[91]

The supremacy of American golf was vividly demonstrated in the 1929 British Open. Hagen won, and eight of the ten leaders were American professionals. Although the British did win the Ryder Cup, it was their first and last victory in these matches, until 1957 when they were victorious again.[92]

In 1930, Jones accomplished the greatest feat in the history of golf — the grand slam. He won the British Amateur, the British Open, the U.S. Open, and the U.S. Amateur in that order. Four major championships in a single year. At the end of the year, Jones announced his retirement from tournament competition.

The number of golf courses in the U.S. reached a record of 5,700 in 1931, including 4,450 private clubs, over 500 municipal courses, and 700 privately owned public fee courses. There were an estimated 9,000 courses throughout the world, of which 2,000 were in the British Empire.[93]

The Royal and Ancient Golf Club of St. Andrews approved the use of steel-shafted golf clubs in 1931. Previously, only hickory or wood-shafted clubs were legal in British championships.[94]

This same period marked the rise of the miniature golf course. It started in Chattanooga, Tennessee, and rapidly spread throughout the U.S. Garnet Carter is reputed to be the inventor of these Tom Thumb courses, which required the use of only the putter. But the rapid rise of miniature golf was exceeded only by the swiftness of its decline.[95]

Walter C. Hagen, Thomas Henry Cotton, of Great Britain, and Leo Diegel preparing to tee off in the Los Angeles Open in 1929. (Photo by courtesy of David Scott Chisholm)

Bobby Jones and Cyril J. H. Tolley at Pebble Beach in 192? preparing to play in the U.S. Amateur Championship. Cyril of Great Britain, had won the British Amateur earlier in the year and was here in an attempt to capture the American Amateur Championship. He did however go to the semifinals losing to Dr. O. F. Willing, the eventual finalist. On the other hand, Bobby Jones lost in the very first round to Johnny Goodman. (Photo by David Scott Chisholm)

The 1930 United States Walker Cup Team which trounced the British Team in May at the Royal St. George's Golf Club, England. Left to right, standing: George Von Elm, Don Moe, Roland MacKenzie, and Bobby Jones. Sitting: Harrison Johnston, Francis Ouimet, Dr. Oscar F. Willing, and George J. Voigt. (Photo by courtesy of the United States Golf Association)

The 1930 British Walker Cup Team comprising Rex W. Hartley, Sir Ernest W. E. Holderness, John N. Smith, T. A. Torrance, James A. Stout, Cyril J. H. Tolley, Roger H. Wethered, and William Campbell. (Photo by courtesy of the United States Golf Association)

An epic scene of the famous "Home Hole" of the Royal and Ancient Golf Club of St. Andrews. This photo was taken by the wife of Bobby Jones, Mary, from the Grand Hotel during one of Bobby's early rounds in the British Amateur Championship in 1930, the "Grand Slam" year. (Photo by courtesy of David Scott Chisholm)

Bobby Jones, finding his ball in the world's most famed hazard, the Swilcan Burn, which guards the first hole of the old course of the Royal and Ancient Golf Club of St. Andrews. Bobby got out of this trouble in noble fashion and finally got his par four. It was in the Amateur event and the first of his four victories for the Grand Slam! (Photo by Courtesy of David Scott Chisholm)

William St. Clair of Roslin, captain of the Honorable Company of Edinburgh Golfers, 1761, 1766, 1770, and 1771. This golf club is the oldest in the world. It was established in 1744 but it did not remain in continual existence. It was deactivated in 1831 then re-established in 1836 and has continued since that time. (Photo by courtesy of the Royal Edinburgh Golf Club. Portrait by George Chalmers) Caption from Nevin H. Gibson, *The Encyclopedia of Golf*. A. S. Barnes & Co., 1958

BLACKHEATH 1876

Medal Day at the Blackheath Golf Club, near London, England. The Royal Blackheath Golf Club is the oldest golf club in England. It was customary to wear the club's red coat on Medal day. (Photo by courtesy of the Royal Blackheath Golf Club. Oil Painting by F. P. Halikins) Caption from W. E. Hughes, *Chronicles of Blackheath Golfers*, Chapman & Hall, 1897.

1750 — Bruntsfield Links
Early days of golf at the Bruntsfield Links, Edinburgh, Scotland. (Photo by courtesy of Donald Teacher, Glasgow, Scotland)

CADDIE WILLIE
William Gunn at the Bruntsfield Links, near Edinburgh, Scotland. (Oil painting by unknown artist, 1838. By courtesy of the Blackheath G.C.)

The British spectators, perhaps the most reserved and nonchalant of all nations, express their excitement most vividly in this panoramic view of the old St. Andrews Golf Course. It was during Bobby Jones' match against Roger Wethered in the British Amateur event in 1930, enroute to winning the first leg of his Grand Slam. (Photo by courtesy of David Scott Chisholm)

A beauteous scene of Bobby Jones putting on the last green in the finals of the British Amateur Championship in 1930. It was the first of his four major championships for the year, which became known as the Grand Slam. The Royal and Ancient Club House, in the background, was constructed in 1854. Within its walls are priceless trophies and photographs guarded like the crown jewels of old England and Scotland. It is referred to as the spiritual home of all golfers. (Photo by courtesy of Bertram Eary of Great Britain)

Bobby Jones putting at Hoylake in the 1930 British Open Championship where he won the second of his four major championships of that year. (Photo by courtesy of David Scott Chisholm)

Leo Diegel, left and big Archie Compston, right, get together in front of the professionals' refreshment tent at the British Open in 1930 at Hoylake. Professionals were forbidden to enter the clubhouses in England during this period. In this event, Leo was tied for second place with Macdonald Smith, while Archie was tied for sixth place with Jim Barnes. (Photo by courtesy of David Scott Chisholm)

3

1931 Through 1949

Robert Elsing Harlow became the manager of the Professional Golfers Association of America in 1929 and he controlled the Tournament Bureau department. In 1921 Bob became the manager of both Walter Hagen and Joe Kirkwood. In this capacity he served as "ghost and Boswell" to the immortal "Haig" through his career, and he continued to lead the Tournament Bureau through the dark Depression. He crossed the Atlantic 23 times to support and promote international golf and his ventures proved extremely successful. He managed the first U.S. Ryder Cup squad to invade Great Britain in 1929 and subsequent teams. He brought Jose Jurado from Argentina to tour with Hagen. He was "guide" for a group of touring Japanese professionals, the first to be seen in this nation. In the 1930's he even imported Mexican caddies, who, at the time, were the best golfers in that nation, to show their wares in California. In June of 1947 he conceived and originated the *Golf World* magazine and published it every week which became the first and only golf newspaper. He prevailed upon John Jay Hopkins to produce the now classic Canada Cup, setting forth promotional aims and ideals; he campaigned for the USGA to inaugurate a Senior Amateur Championship and now both men and women play for national titles in this category.[96] In 1954, Bob Harlow and his great friend, Grantland

Rice, bid the golfing world a farewell for greener courses. The *Golf World* magazine is still flourishing under the capable guidance of Bob's wife, Mrs. Lillian Harlow.

From 1931 to 1935, the club members of the U.S.G.A. dropped from a record 1,154 to 767, many of them victims of the Depression. At the same time, many, many tournaments cut the prize purse and some were completely suspended.

But a turn for the better came in 1936, when the executive committee of the U.S.G.A. reported an increased membership. Further, the association took larger executive quarters and began the preparation of a golf museum.[97]

The Professional Golfers Association of America also made an encouraging report when it was announced that the professionals were to compete for over $100,000 during the year. Freddy Corcoran was appointed tournament director, succeeding Robert Harlow.[98]

After Bobby Jones retired in 1931, new names and some old names appeared in the headlines. Francis Ouimet, who had risen to the height of international fame in 1913 when he won the U.S. Open, captured his second U.S. Amateur title 18 years later at Chicago. Then Walter Hagen came through to win his first Canadian Open Championship, giving the old master every major and semi-

Robert E. Harlow, manager of Walter Hagen, the first P.G.A. Tournament Director and the Founder of *Golf World* Magazine. (Photo by courtesy of Mrs. Lillian E. Harlow, *Golf World* Magazine)

Francis Ouimet returns to the scene and wins his second U.S. Amateur Championship after 17 years, at the Beverly C. C., Chicago, in 1931. Least forgotten was his great triumph of 1913 when he as an unknown amateur defeated the great immortals Harry Vardon and Ted Ray in a playoff to win the U.S. Open Championship at Brookline. (Photo by courtesy of David Scott Chisholm)

Billy Burke sinking final putt in the United States Open Championship 72-hole playoff at the Inverness Club, Toledo, Ohio, 1931. (Photo by courtesy of the United States Golf Asociation)

Francis Ouimet putting on 18th green during his match with Jack Westland in the finals of the Amateur Championship at the Beverly Country Club, Chicago, 1931. (Photo by courtesy of the United States Golf Association)

Tommy D. Armour, who learned his golf at Braid Hills, Edinburgh, Scotland, entered the British Open from the U.S.A., and emerged victorious, which, according to his own confession, was his greatest moment. Seen here receiving the Open Trophy from the Earl of Airlie at Carnoustie in 1931. The "Silver Scot" has now won every major championship under the sun — the U.S. Open Championship, the National P.G.A. Championship, and the British Open Championship. (Photo by courtesy of Bertram Eary of Great Britain)

major golf title under the sun. Tommy Armour won the British Open. The "transplanted Scot" went to his native heath, Carnoustie, to win the only major championship in which he had previously been deprived. During the same year, Billie Burke defeated the great amateur, George Von Elm, in a double playoff to win the U.S. Open Championship.[99]

In 1932, the U.S.G.A. instituted the first international women's amateur matches between Great Britain and the U.S. These became the Curtis Cup matches in honor of Harriot and Margaret Curtis. The U.S. team won the first match at Wentworth, England, 5½ to 3½.[100]

The same year, Gene Sarazen reappeared when he captured both the British Open Championship and the U.S. National Open. Hagen won his fifth Western Open, which was to be his last big championship.

The famed Masters tournament, sponsored by the Augusta National Golf Club in Augusta, Georgia, was inaugurated in 1934. Bobby Jones, in conjunction with Dr. Alister MacKenzie, spent many months in planning this beautiful course over the grounds which formerly comprised a nursery. The project began in 1931, when Jones and his friends purchased the 365-acre tract at a depression price. Horton Smith won the first Masters tournament with 284, beating Craig Wood by a stroke.[101]

Max Baer (Heavyweight), and Walter Hagen on the tee at Sacramento, California. (Photo by courtesy of David Scott Chisholm)

Babe Ruth, the "Homerun King" and admired by every American boy, follows through at the Rancho Golf Club in Los Angeles. The Babe is using the recently introduced "Wedge," a modified niblic. (Photo by courtesy of David Scott Chisholm)

A close-up of Billie Burke, U.S. Open winner of 1931. (Photo by courtesy of David Scott Chisholm)

W. Lawson Little, Jr., won both the U.S. National Amateur and the British Amateur in 1934, scoring what became known as the "little slam." Even more remarkable, he successfully defended both titles in 1935. Little, the longest driver in the game at the time, turned professional and in 1936 he won the Canadian Open Championship. In 1940, he defeated Gene Sarazen in a playoff for the U.S. National Open title.

The late 1930's also brought to the fore the names of such pros as Byron Nelson, Sam Snead, Ben Hogan, Ralph Guldahl, Denny Shute, Craig Wood, Jimmy Thomson, Paul Runyan, Harry Cooper, Henry Picard, John Revolta, Jimmy Demaret, and a host of others.

Pro golf became big business, and the social stature of the professional golfer rose proportionately. Walter Hagen, who by this time had aged out of competitive golf, did much along these lines. The Haig tore down many barriers which restricted the social freedom of the pros. Among other things, the Haig, was the first pro to earn and spend a million dollars. During the course of his worldwide ventures, he received privileged recognition which obviously broke down certain barriers to which pros were previously subjected.[102] The pros of today will always be indebted to the fabulous Haig.

Larger purses came with the increasing number of tournaments in which they could compete. The small $2,500 purses were a thing of the past, and when such events were sectionally sponsored, only the local pros played in them for the good of the club with which they were affiliated.

With improved steel-shafted clubs, golf balls, sand wedge, and better golf courses and green management, the golfers were scoring better. In 1938, the U.S.G.A. limited the number of golf clubs to 14.[103]

The "Fabulous Haig" with one of his many admirers. Palm Springs, California. (Photo by courtesy of David Scott Chisholm)

The Haig won his fifth Western Open title in 1932. He is seen here eating his birthday cake. Walter was born December 21, 1892. (Photo by courtesy of David Scott Chisholm)

Walter Hagen, in semi-retirement, still draws a gallery. He plays only in selected events. His 11 major championships is a professional record. (Photo by courtesy of David Scott Chisholm)

Walter Hagen and A. K. Bourne during a friendly round in a "Pull Cart." (Photo by courtesy of David Scott Chisholm)

Gene Sarazen sinks the final putt for a record round of 66, giving him a record tying total of 286 to win the U.S. Open Championship at the Fresh Meadow C. C., N. Y., in 1932. Gene played the last 28 holes in 100 strokes. He had just won the British Open earlier in the year. These two victories made him the second man, after Jones, to win both the U.S. Open and the British Open during the same year. (Photo by courtesy of Gene Sarazen. *Thirty Years of Championship Golf*, Prentice Hall, 1950)

Three amateur golfers, but professionals in the cinema field, talking things over in Hollywood. Left to right: Douglas Fairbanks, Adolph Menjou, and George Marshall. The latter directed the Bobby Jones series of motion pictures in 1931. (Photo by courtesy of David Scott Chisholm)

Joe Kirkwood, Sr., the greatest trick shot artist ever known. Joe could do more than just tricks, he knew how to play winning golf. In 1933 he won both the Canadian Open and the North and South Open Championships. A great friend and traveling companion of Walter Hagen, they traveled around the world together to exhibit their golfing abilities. (Photo by courtesy of David Scott Chisholm)

Leo Diegel using his internationally known putting stance at the Wilshire Country Club during the 1932 Los Angeles Open Championship. (Photo by courtesy of David Scott Chisholm)

Lawson Little and James Wallace walking in after the British Amateur Championship finals at Prestwick in 1934. Lawson was victorious and he also won the U.S. National Amateur Championship the same year. In the following year, 1935, Lawson repeated both victories which gave him two consecutive "Little Slams." (Photo by courtesy of Bertram Eary of Great Britain)

Miss Virginia Van Wie, of the Beverly Country Club, Chicago, won her third consecutive U.S. Women's Amateur Championship in 1934 at the Whitemarsh Valley Country Club, near Philadelphia. In the finals she defeated Mrs. Dorothy Traung by 2 & 1. It was to be her last championship as Virginia declared her retirement from competitive play shortly afterwards. (Photo by courtesy of David Scott Chisholm)

Johnny Revolta, winner of the National P.G.A. Championship in 1935 at Oklahoma City. Johnny also won the Western Open in the same year. (Photo by courtesy of Wilson Sporting Goods)

Gene Sarazen demonstrating the club and the swing with which he scored the double eagle in order to win the Masters in 1935. Gene hit his second shot on the par five, 15th hole and it rolled into the hole for his double eagle and enabled him to tie Craig Wood. He then won the playoff which gave him seven major victories. The Masters, instituted in 1934 is played at the Augusta National Golf Club and was instituted by the immortal Robert T. Jones, Jr. (Photo by courtesy of David Scott Chisholm)

T. Henry Cotton, the great professional from England, is seen driving at Sandwich in 1934 where he was victorious in the British Open Championship with a record-tying score of 283. The invading American professionals had carried away the British trophy for ten consecutive years prior to Cotton's victory. (Photo by courtesy of Bertram Eary of Great Britain)

Sam Parks, Jr., became the darkest of all horses when he won the U.S. Open Championship in 1935 at Oakmont, Pa. (Photo by David Scott Chisholm)

Paul "Poison" Runyon won the National P.G.A. Championship at Williamsville, N. Y., when he defeated Craig Wood on the 38th hole during the final match. Paul also won the North and South Open on two occasions, in 1930 and 1935. (Photo by courtesy of David Scott Chisholm)

Pamela Barton proudly exhibits the British Ladies' Amateur trophy which she won in 1936. She later captured the U.S. Women's Amateur to become the second woman to win both events in one year. Pamela, who won the British Ladies' event again in 1939, was killed in action while serving in the British WAAFS, just shortly after winning her third major title. (Photo by courtesy of D. M. Mathieson, *Golf Monthly*, Edinburgh, Scotland)

The 1936 Walker Cup Teams of Great Britain and the United States. The British amateurs are on the left and the Americans on the right. These matches were played at the Pine Valley Country Club, Clementon, N. J., and the U.S. Team was victorious with a runaway score of nine to naught.

THE BRITISH TEAM	THE U.S. TEAM
Hector Thomson	John G. Goodman
Jack McLean	Albert E. Campbell
R. Cecil Ewing	John W. Fischer
G. Alec Hill	Reynolds Smith
Gordon B. Peters	Walter Emery
J. Morton Dykes	Charles R. Yates
Harry G. Bentley	George T. Dunlap
John D. A. Langley	Ed White
CAPTAIN —	CAPTAIN —
Dr. William Tweddell	Francis D. Ouimet

(Photo by courtesy of the U.S. Golf Association)

Jimmy Thompson, from North Berwick, Scotland and now an American professional, is the longest hitter known. He was runner-up in the National P.G.A. Championship in 1936 at Pinehurst, N. C., to Denny Shute. (Photo by courtesy of David Scott Chisholm)

The Professional Golfers Association announced the award of the first Vardon Trophy in 1937 to Harry Cooper. Named in honor of the British star, Harry Vardon, the trophy is awarded to the professional having the finest tournament record.[104] (Since 1947, the trophy has been awarded to the pro having the lowest scoring average.) Heretofore, it was awarded on a point basis.

Ralph Guldahl came to the fore in 1937 and 1939, during which years he won two consecutive U.S. Open titles and was the runner-up in the Masters Tournament. Guldahl also won three consecutive Western Open titles, for a record which still stands today.

All U.S.G.A. tournaments were cancelled in 1942 after America's entry into World War II. However, a number of open and amateur events continued. Ben Hogan ended the year as the leading money winner for the third consecutive year, followed by Byron Nelson and Sam Snead.

Macdonald Smith, one of the greatest uncrowned kings of golf. This chip shot won him $1500 in the Los Angeles Open. Macdonald was runner-up in the British Open for the third time in 1932. In 1930 he was runner-up in the U.S. Open Championship. Although he won his share of regular tournaments, he never captured a major championship. (Photo by courtesy of David Scott Chisholm)

A close-up of Denny Shute, winner of two consecutive P.G.A. Championships in 1936 and 1937. Denny also won the British Open Championship in 1933 after a playoff against another American, Craig Wood. (Photo by courtesy of Wilson Sporting Goods)

A group of outstanding professionals who made an indelible mark in the history of American golf during the early portion of the 1930's. From right to left are Leo Diegel, Paul Runyon, "Lighthorse" Harry Cooper, Macdonald Smith, Horton Smith, Craig Wood, Johnny Revolta, Denny Shute, Tom Creavy and "Lord" Byron Nelson. This group has won no less than 20 major championships. (Photo by courtesy of David Scott Chisholm)

A 'Trio' of great contributors to the game. Macdonald Smith, Bing Crosby and Walter Hagen. (Photo by courtesy of David Scott Chisholm)

Joyce Wethered, now Lady Heathcoat-Amory, president of the English Ladies' Golf Association. She won the British Ladies' Championship on four occasions from 1922 to 1929. Of all the very famous women golfers she is hailed as the greatest during the 1920's by Bobby Jones. The Heathcoat-Amorys are one of the most powerful and wealthy industrial families in England. (Photo by courtesy of David Scott Chisholm)

Johnny Goodman of Omaha, who won the U.S. Open Championship in 1933, added the U.S. Amateur title to his credit in 1937 at the Alderwood Country Club, Portland, Oregon. He defeated Ray Billows in the final round by 2 up. Johnny's name first came fore in 1929 when he upset the immortal Bobby Jones in the first round of the U.S. Amateur Championship at Pebble Beach, California. (Photo by courtesy of David Scott Chisholm)

Byron Nelson in 1937, the year he won the Masters Tournament and showed signs of an up-and-coming immortal professional. In later years he was to become the favorite in every event he entered. (Photo by courtesy of David Scott Chisholm)

Sam Snead from the hills of West Virginia came forward in 1937 and 1938 to win 14 championships. In 1938 his nine titles, all P.G.A. events, made him the leading money winner of the year. His name was to appear again. (Photo by courtesy of David Scott Chisholm)

The first British team to win the Walker Cup (1938). The above British Walker Cup team was the first and, so far, the only team ever to win the Walker Cup for Great Britain. Back row, left to right: G. B. Peters, H. Thomson, L. G. Crawley, A. T. Kyle, and J. J. F. Pennink. Front row: H. G. Bentley, C. Ewing, J. B. Beck (Captain), C. Stowe, and J. Bruen, Jr. They won at the famed St. Andrews course by seven to four. (Photo by courtesy of D. M. Mathieson, *Golf Monthly*, Edinburgh, Scotland)

The war years of golf were the era of Byron Nelson. In 1944, Nelson won no less than 13 of the 23 tournaments and was the year's leading money winner with a record of $37,967.69. Harold "Jug" McSpaden followed with $23,855.30.

Nelson and McSpaden, who became known as the "Gold Dust" twins, marched in with approximately $100,000 in 1945. "Lord Byron" himself collected $63,335.66 and McSpaden $36,299.18. Out of 38 tournaments held in 1945, Nelson participated in 31. He won 17 and was runner-up in 7. His average was a record 68.33 strokes per round. Starting in Miami on March 8, Nelson launched a string of consecutive victories which has never been approached in the history of the game. After his Miami victory, Nelson swept 11 consecutive tournaments, including the National PGA and the Canadian Open. His march of triumph lasted from

March 8 to August 4. The richest event was the Tam O'Shanter, in which he won $13,600 and finished 13 strokes ahead of Ben Hogan and Gene Sarazen.[105]

With the end of the war, the Professional Golfers Association announced that the professionals would compete in at least 45 tournaments in 1946. A minimum purse of $10,000 for each event was established. The total cash awards would amount to about $600,000.[106]

Women professionals entered the scene in 1946 when a small group held its first Open championship at Spokane, Washington. Patty Berg defeated Betty Jameson in a match play event and won the prize of $5,600 in war bonds.

By the end of 1946, many of the pre-war leaders returned and were reaping large harvests. Ben Hogan had won his first major title, the National PGA

Championship, and was the leading money winner of the year for the fourth time. Lloyd Mangrum, a newcomer, had won the U.S. Open after a three-way playoff. Sam Snead won the British Open Championshop.

Ben Hogan rose to the top again in 1948. He ended the year as the leading money winner for the fifth time and won two more major championships — the U.S. Open and the National PGA Championship. He also won the Western Open Championship.

The U.S.G.A. instituted the Junior Amateur Championship for boys in 1948 and one year later started the amateur for girls.[107] The USGA abandoned the stymie rule in 1950 but the R&A Golf Club retained it.[108]

"Wee" Bobby Cruikshank escaped from more than one German prison during World War I, then came to America and achieved national fame in the golfing world. In 1923 he lost in a playoff to Bobby Jones for the U.S. National Open title. He was the leading money winner in 1927. (Photo by courtesy of David Scott Chisholm)

Study of a stymie. Marvin Ward on the 28th green in the final match with Raymond Billows in the 1939 Amateur Championship at the North Shore Country Club, Glenview, Ill. He negotiated the stymie with a mashie-niblick, halved the hole, and later won the match. (Photo by courtesy of the United States Golf Association)

Ralph Guldahl putting and winning the U.S. Open Championship. Within a span of three years, from 1936 to 1939, Ralph won three major titles and three consecutive Western Open Championships. His majors were two consecutive U.S. Open Championships and the Masters Tournament. A native of Dallas, Texas, Ralph also won the Radix Trophy in 1936. In the following year, the Radix Trophy was replaced with the Vardon Trophy, so named after the immortal British Professional, Harry Vardon. (Photo by courtesy of Ed Dudley)

Ben Hogan at Oak Hill C.C., Rochester, N.Y. in 1940. Ben won four tournaments that year and ended as the leading money winner. (Photo by courtesy of Bruce Koch, Rochester, N.Y.)

124

Henry Picard won one of the most thrilling of all P.G.A. Championships when he defeated the reigning U.S. Open champion, Byron Nelson, in the final round on the 37th hole, in 1939 at Flushing, N.Y. Henry also ended the year as the leading money winner. (Photo by courtesy of David Scott Chisholm)

Craig Wood's hour finally arrived in 1941 when he won the U.S. Open Championship and in the same year, the Masters Tournament. Craig had previously been a runner-up in *five* major championships. In the Open at the Colonial C.C., Fort Worth, Texas, the rain was so heavy and the lightning so severe during the second round that play was twice stopped. (Photo by courtesy of David Scott Chisholm)

Byron Nelson

"Lord" Byron Nelson while at the top of his form. The former Fort Worth caddy broke or shattered every record in the book from 1936 through 1946. Even after his semi-retirement in 1946, he continued to make golf history. (Photo by courtesy of MacGregor, Cincinnati, Ohio)

Lieutenant Nevin H. Gibson, the compiler, poses in Scottish kilts while in Scotland in 1943. It was during this year in which he commenced to compile the data for *The Encyclopedia of Golf*. Some of this same material is contained in this volume. (Photo by courtesy of Renfield, Edinburgh, Scotland)

126

Lloyd Mangram emerged as a top contender immediately after the war. In 1946 he won the U.S. National Open Championship in Cleveland after a three-way playoff against Byron Nelson and Victor Ghezzi. Seen here executing a trap shot without removing his cigarette, a Mangrum characteristic. Mangrum was the first professional golfer to own and fly his own airplane from tournament to tournament. (David Scott Chisholm)

A smiling Byron Nelson, with every reason to do so. From 1936 through 1946, Lord Byron won no less than 50 championships. His biggest year was 1945. During that year 38 tournaments were held: Nelson played in 31, won 17, and was runner-up in 7. He won a string of 11 consecutive tournaments, a record which has never been approached. His average round for the year was another record, 68.33. He ended the year as the leading money winner once again with another record of $63,335.66. Unfortunately, Nelson was at the zenith of his form during the war years when all USGA tournaments and the Masters were discontinued He went into semi-retirement in 1946 (Photo by courtesy of David Scott Chisholm)

Jock Hutchison of Chicago was born at St. Andrews, Scotland, and went back to win the British Open at his home course in 1921. He won it after a playoff with Roger Wethered, a British amateur. Seen here some 20-odd years later, retaining his most rhythmical swing. (Photo by courtesy of David Scott Chisholm)

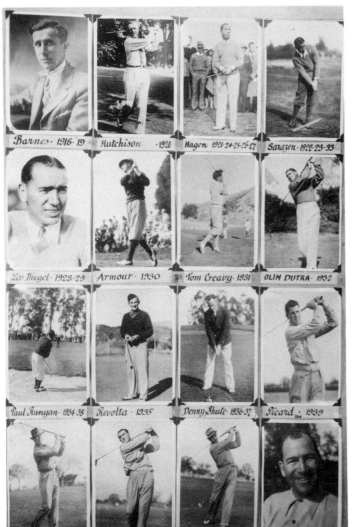

The 16 winners of the National PGA Championship since the tournament began in 1916, showing the winners up to 1945. Hagen won a record five. Sam Snead was the only one among this group to capture a major title after 1945. Hogan won his first National PGA Championship in 1946. (Photo by courtesy of David Scott Chisholm)

The entrance to the clubhouse of the Augusta National Golf Club, the venue for the Masters Tournament. Taken from the magnolia lane, the main thru-fare where the contestants and leading officials enter. (Photo by Nevin H. Gibson)

The Firestone Country Club, Akron, Ohio, the venue for the World Series of Golf and CBS Golf Classic. In 1966 the Firestone C.C., sponsored the National PGA Championship on their course. (Photo by Nevin H. Gibson)

Gary Player — 1962 at Aronimink C.C., Philadelphia, Pa.

Jack Nicklaus — 1963 at Dallas Athletic C.C., Dallas, Texas

Bobby Nichols — 1964 Columbus C.C., Columbus, Ohio

Dave Marr — 1965 Laurel Valley G.C., Ligonier, Pa.

Although these professionals are practicing at the Augusta National Golf Club, they are the winners of four consecutive National PGA Championships. (Photos by Nevin H. Gibson)

Practicing that most important stroke, "The Putt," on the practice putting green of the Augusta National golf course, tuning up for the Masters Tournament of 1966. (Photo by Nevin H. Gibson)

Gardiner Dickinson.

Doug Sanders, blue shoes & sweater

Sam Snead

Billy Casper

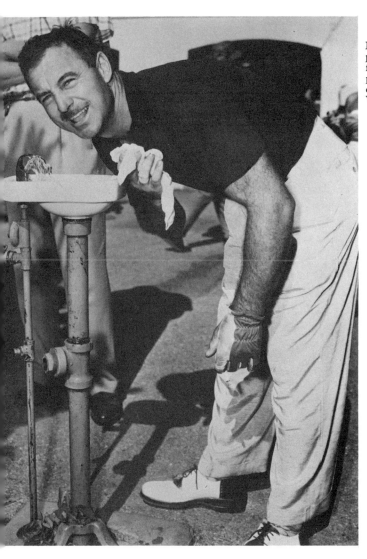

Robert "Skee" Riegel, winner of the U.S. Amateur Championship in 1947. "Skee" defeated Johnny Dawson of California at Pebble Beach in the finals by 2 & 1. He became a professional in 1950. He is referred to as "Popeye" in view of his giant forearms, as seen here. (Photo by courtesy of Wilson Sporting Goods Co., Chicago, Ill.)

Lew Worsham, winner of the U.S. Open Championship at St. Louis in 1947 after a playoff against Sam Snead. In the playoff both Sam and Lew played sub-par golf and the match was nip and tuck. On the last green, Sam proceeded to sink a putt of less than a yard for his 69. However, Lew intervened and requested that the two putts be measured to determine which ball was away. Sam's ball was away and he missed for a 70. Lew sank for a winning 69. Some years later, 1953, Lew holed a wedge shot on the last green at the Tam O'Shanter World's Championship for an eagle two (the shot that was heard around the world), which gave him the first prize of $25,000 as he won by a single stroke. (Photo by courtesy of David Scott Chisholm)

Joe Louis, former World's Heavyweight Champion, is a very avid golfer. Joe shoots in the 70's and plays frequently in the Los Angeles area.

John Weissmuller, former world's champion swimmer and Tarzan of the movies, lines up a putt. John is a fine amateur and plays frequently in Southern California. (Photo by courtesy of David Scott Chisholm)

130

An outstanding threesome: Horton Smith, past PGA prexy and twice Masters champion; Herb Graffis, Golfing and Golfdom; and the "Fabulous" Walter Hagen, winner of 11 major championships. Their subject — *Golf*. (Photo by courtesy of Wilson Sporting Goods Co., Chicago, Ill.)

Mrs. (Babe Didrikson) George Zaharias who in 1947 became the first American golfer to win the British Ladies' Amateur Championship. One year earlier, she won the U S. Women's Championship. In 1932 she was hailed as the greatest woman athlete alive. Then she took to golf and reached the top in dazzling fashion. (Photo by courtesy of David Scott Chisholm)

The royalty watches the Royal and Ancient Sport. Here we see His Majesty King George VI as a spectator at the British Open Championship in 1948 at Muirfield. (Photo by courtesy of *Golf Monthly*, Great Britain)

The 1947 U.S. Ryder Cup team, *left to right,* top row: E. J. Harrison, Lloyd Mangrum, Herman Keiser, Byron Nelson, and Sam Snead. Bottom: Herman Barron, Jimmy Demaret, captain Ben Hogan, Ed Oliver, and Lew Worsham. (Photo by courtesy of Robert A. Hudson, Portland, Oregon)

133

The 1947 British Ryder Cup team, *left to right,* back row:
Commander R.C.T. Roe, R.N.R. Secretary British PGA.,
James Adams, Max Faulkner, Eric Green, Charles Ward and
Reg Horne. Front row: Sam King, Fred Daly, captain Henry
Cotton, Dai Rees, and Arthur Lees. (Photo by courtesy of
Robert A. Hudson, Portland, Oregon)

T. Henry Cotton, the greatest British professional since Harry Vardon, won his third British Open title in 1948 at Muirfield with a 284, five strokes in the lead. Henry is a great student of the sport and has since written several outstanding golf books. He is also one of the best teachers in the game. (Photo by courtesy of David Scott Chisholm)

William Benjamin Hogan reaped his greatest harvest in 1948 as evidenced by the winning trophies on hand. Left to right are the National PGA trophy, the U.S. Open trophy and the Western Open trophy. Just a few months later he was involved in a most serious auto accident which almost cost him his life. But in defiance of the doctors, Ben came back again to become one of the greatest golfers of all times.

Louise Suggs, one of the top echelon woman golfers, proudly displays the U.S. Women's Amateur trophy and the British Ladies' Amateur trophy. She won the latter in 1948 and became the second American golfer to do so. (Louise later turned pro-ette. (Photo by courtesy of MacGregor Co., Cincinnati, Ohio)

No golfer ever lived who practiced more than Ben Hogan. Ben suffered many lean years in the game and even gave it up temporarily. But he came back to pursue the profession to which he had devoted so much time. His return was again a rough road to travel. However, he finally found the answer, where he thought it was all the time, *on the practice tee*. In this game of golf, like many other things, "What so ever a man giveth, he shall also receive." (Photo by courtesy of David Scott Chisholm)

Bobby Locke from South Africa holds the British Open trophy which he won for the first time in 1949. Locke was a sensation in the U.S. in the late 1940's, shortly after the war as he was one of the leading money winners. He later won a total of four British Open Championships and countless other championships all over the world. Although Bobby never won a major title in the U.S., he was very close to the top in three consecutive U.S. Opens from 1947 through 1949. (Photo by courtesy of D. M. Mathieson, *Golf Monthly*)

Sam Urzetta driving off the 14th tee at Oak Hll Country Club, Rochester, N.Y., durng the 1949 U.S. Natonal Amateur Championship. Sam lost in the 5th round to Charles B. Dudley by one down. In the following year, 1950, Sam was more successful. He defeated Frank Stranahan in the finals on the 39th hole at Minneapolis Golf Club, Minn. (Photo by courtesy of Bruce Koch, Rochester, N.Y.)

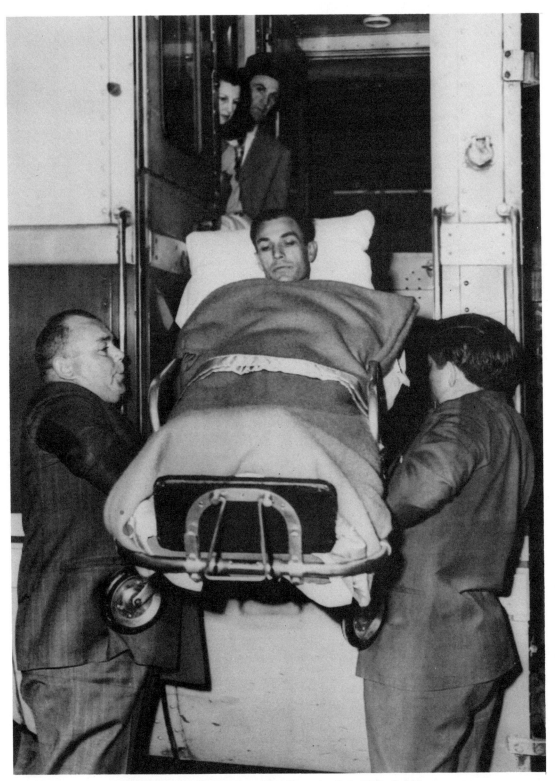

Ben Hogan arrives at Fort Worth on April 2, 1949, finishing
a trip which started February 2. Ben and his wife Valerie,
seen in the background, were involved in an auto-bus crash
near Van Horn, Texas. Here Ben is being removed from
train. (Photo by courtesy of Bruce Koch, Rochester, N.Y.)

Sam Urzetta, the U.S. National Amateur Champion in 1950. Sam defeated the favorite, Frank Stranahan, son of a wealthy industrialist, in a record overtime final match on the 39th hole. Stranahan, earlier, had won his second British Amateur title and was by far the big favorite. (Photo by courtesy of Wilson Sporting Goods Co., Chicago, Ill.)

A rear view of clubhouse of the Augusta National Golf Club, and the home of the Masters Tournament which the immortal Bobby Jones instituted in 1934. (Photo by courtesy of Ed Dudley)

A bird's eye view of the action in the U.S. Amateur Championship of 1949 at Oak Hill Country Club, N.Y. Charlie Coe, the eventual winner, is seen preparing to putt. (Photo courtesy of Bruce Koch, N.Y.)

Johnny Dawson concedes match to Charlie Coe on the 21st hole at Oak Hill C.C., after missing a short putt in the quarterfinals. Coe finally won the 1949 U.S. Amateur Championship when he defeated Rugus King in the finals by a record margin of 11 and 10. (Photo by courtesy of Bruce Koch, Rochester, N.Y.)

4

1950 Through the Present

The year 1949 was the greatest for Samuel Jackson Snead. He won his first Masters Tournament, the National PGA Championship, the Western Open, the North and South Open, the Vardon trophy, and was the year's leading money winner. He was also tied for runner-up in the U.S. Open Championship.[109]

The name of Hogan continued to dominate the game in the 1950's despite an auto accident in 1949 that almost took his life. Still limping from injuries, Hogan was a surprise entrant in the 1950 Los Angeles Open, where the purse had been increased to $15,000. After an opening round of 73, Hogan scored three successive 69's and looked like the winner until Sam Snead sank a long curling putt on the last green to tie. Ben lost the playoff, but the important thing was that Hogan was back. Next, he entered the Masters and finished in a tie with Byron Nelson for fourth place. Perhaps he reserved his best for the biggest — the U.S. Open — at Ardmore, Pa. At the end of four rounds, the gallant little Texan was tied with Lloyd Mangrum and George Fazio. He won the playoff on sheer determination and courage. It was a high point in one of golf's most poignant comebacks.

Hogan continued his mastery in 1951 when he won his first Masters Tournament and successfully defended his U.S. Open title and the world's championship. But it was in 1953 that Hogan carved out the greatest triumphs of his career, winning the three leading championships of the world.

Hogan started the year at the Augusta National Golf Club, where he again won the Masters Tournament, this time with a record 274.

His next victory was in the Pan-American Open. He followed this with a victory at his native Fort Worth, Texas, where he won the Colonial National with a 282. Then came the U.S. National Open at rugged Oakmont, where the little man was victorious for his fourth time. His score broke the course record and he was six strokes in front of Sam Snead, the second place finisher. Hogan now turned his sights on the British Open at the ancient windswept links of Carnoustie, Scotland, which required a peculiar brand of golf with a smaller ball to which Ben was not accustomed. It was his first attempt and he again made history. He opened with a 73 and improved with each round until he scored a final 68 for a 282 to win by four strokes. Yes, it was another record for the Carnoustie course and when he made his last putt on the 72nd green, for his assured victory, there were tears of happiness in the eyes of the golfing world. He had now won every major championship of the world.[110]

It was assumed that Hogan would retire from competitive golf after his great victories of 1953,

An autographed photo of "Flashy" Jimmy Demaret. The colorful professional also put his autograph on three Master titles and became the first in history to achieve this feat. His third victory came in 1950 when he gained seven strokes on the last six holes to defeat Jim Ferrier by two strokes. (Photo by courtesy of the MacGregor Co., Cincinnati, Ohio)

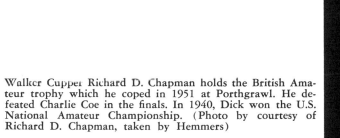

Walker Cupper Richard D. Chapman holds the British Amateur trophy which he coped in 1951 at Porthgrawl. He defeated Charlie Coe in the finals. In 1940, Dick won the U.S. National Amateur Championship. (Photo by courtesy of Richard D. Chapman, taken by Hemmers)

Robert A. Hudson, Sr., of Portland, Oregon, whose efforts as Chairman of the National Advisory Committee have been an inspiration to the officers of the P.G.A. of America. Mr. Hudson sponsored the Ryder Cup Matches in 1947, also the National PGA Championship in 1946. (Photo by courtesy of Robert A. Hudson, Sr.)

Bing Crosby driving off along with Bob Hope in the rear during their charity match in England in 1952. An immense crowd followed them and much cash was raised for a good cause. Both Bing and Bob have long been avid golfers and have contributed tremendously to the game. (Photo by courtesy of David Scott Chisholm)

Frank Stranahan, outstanding American amateur, accepts the best wishes of James Walker of the Coldstream Guards in the British Amateur Championship at Prestwick in 1952. Walker had lost to Frank the previous day. Frank lost in the final round to his American rival, Harvie Ward. (Photo by courtesy of David Scott Chisholm)

just as Bobby Jones did after the 1930 grand slam. But he had another goal — to become the first and only American to win five U.S. Open Championships.

His first appearance in 1954 was at the Masters, where he tied with Sam Snead for the title. The playoff was sensational. Hogan hit every green in regulation figures while Snead missed five, yet Snead recovered brilliantly and won by a single stroke. Hogan's next move was the Open at Springfield, N. J., but this was Ed Furgol's event and Hogan ended in a tie for sixth.

By now, Hogan was competing in only a few selected tournaments and his next move was at the Masters in 1955, where he was again a runner-up. The same year, he almost reached his coveted goal of a fifth National Open title. In fact, he was congratulated by many who thought he had it in the bag. But an unknown golfer by the name of Jack Fleck, using Hogan clubs, played the last five holes of the Olympic Country Club at San Francisco in two under par, tied Hogan, and defeated him in a playoff. Hogan came close again the following year at Rochester, N. Y., but he missed a 30-inch putt on the 17th hole and finished in a tie for second to Cary Middlecoff.[111]

International golf received another boost in 1952 when the first match for the Americas Cup was held

Julius Boros describes a hole during the final round of the U.S. Open Championship to a sportswriter while walking to the next tee. An unusual procedure in such event, however, it did not seem to bother him or his score as indicated on the placard. Julius is renowned for his coolness and most nonchalant mode of play. (Photo by courtesy of Wilson Sporting Goods, Chicago, Ill.)

Julius Boros executes an excellent explosion in perfect grace. It was this shot that contributed to his victory at Dallas in 1952 when he won the U.S. Open Championship. (Eleven years later, 1963, he won his second U.S. Open title at Brookline, Mass., where he defeated Palmer and Cupit in playoff). (Photo by courtesy of Wilson Sporting Goods, Chicago, Ill.)

Beautious Prestwick Links, Scotland, during the play of the British Amateur Championship in 1952. The British Open was first played over the Prestwick links in 1860 and it remained the venue of the Open until 1873 at which time it was decided to rotate the venue for the Open. (Photo by courtesy of David Scott Chisholm)

Miss Louise Suggs, one of America's finest feminine golfers. The lady from Georgia won her second U.S. Women's Open Championship in 1952 at Philadelphia, with a record score of 284. Louise also has one British Ladies' Amateur title and one U.S. Women's Amateur title. (Photo by courtesy of the MacGregor Company, Cincinnati, Ohio)

Ed (Porky) Oliver jigs for a putt to drop. Ed, one of the favorites of the gallery, was again a runner-up in a major championship in 1953. He was second to Ben Hogan in the Masters and it marked the third time he had ended second in a major event. "Porky" won the Western Open in 1941. (Photo by courtesy of David Scott Chisholm)

The 1953 Ryder Cup Matches were played at Wentworth, England, and the U.S. team defeated their British cousins by a single point. It marked the eighth victory for the U.S., out of ten international matches. The 1953 Ryder Cup team, *left to right,* standing: Jim Turnesa, Walter Burkemo, Freddie Haas, Jr., Dave Douglas, Ed Oliver and Ted Kroll. Sitting: Cary Middlecoff, Lloyd Mangrum, Sam Snead and Jack Burke, Jr. (Photo courtesy of D. M. Mathieson, *Golfers Handbook*)

in Seattle, Washington, between the amateur golfers of Mexico, Canada, and the United States. The Americas Cup was presented by Jerome P. Bowers, Jr., past president of the Western Golf Association.[112] The first Hopkins Cup Matches were also held in 1952, between professionals from Canada and the United States. The late John J. Hopkins was the founder and the president of the International Golf Association, whose aim is to improve international relations through golf.[113]

The United States Golf Association assumed the sponsorship of the Women's Open Championship in 1953 at the request of the Ladies Professional Golfers Association. Betsy Rawls defeated Jacqueline Pung in a playoff to win.[114]

The U.S. Open Championship was televised for the first time in 1954 and prize money was increased by 20 percent. The gallery was the largest ever with 39,600 in attendance. Ed Furgol, handicapped since childhood with a withered left arm, was the winner.[115] The winner of the U.S. Amateur Championship was Arnold Palmer, a name which later became quite famous.

The United States Golf Association established a Senior Amateur Championship in 1955 as a result of the remarkable growth in senior golf. Although the U.S. Seniors' Golf Association was established in 1905, they possessed a substantial waiting list.[116] The U.S.G.A. now conducts a total of eight individual championships each year which is apart from the international matches they sponsor. In the following year, 1956, the U.S.G.A. revised its scale of yards for determining par for the first time since 1917[117]

The National P.G.A. Championship was changed in 1958 from match play to stroke play. Since the activation of this event in 1916, it has always been a match play affair. From the aspect of television, spectators, and a number of other advantages, stroke play, it was felt, is far more beneficial than match

Ben Hogan showing his great form at Carnoustie where he entered in his first British Open Championship in 1953 and won in brilliant style. The spectators in the old country were most anxious to see Ben's performance and he left them with no disappointments. (Photo by courtesy of Bruce Koch, Rochester, N. Y.)

The immortal William Benjamin Hogan holds the famous British Open trophy which he won most courageously in 1953. During the same year he also won his fourth U.S. Open Championship and his second Master's title. It was his first attempt in the British Open which he won in magnificent style with a 282 over the famed Carnoustie course. His victories in 1953 gave the *wee ice mon,* as the Scots called him, a total of nine major victories which included every major championship under the sun. Hogan was the overwhelming choice of the sportscasters as the male athlete of 1953. Such decision was not difficult after Ben, still limping after his almost fatal auto accident, won the triple crown. (Photo by courtesy of D. M. Mathieson, *The Golfers Handbook*)

Arnold Palmer, a product of Wake Forest College, N.C., and a native of Pennsylvania, won the U.S. Amateur Championship in 1954 at Pine Ridge C.C., Cleveland. (He turned professional the following year and his name was to reappear time and time again.) (Photo by courtesy of Wlson Sporting Goods, Chicago, Ill.)

Little Bob Toski won the biggest golf prize in the history of the game up to 1954, during which year he captured the world's championship when the winner's prize was increased to $50.000. This tremendous sum enabled Bob to become the leading money winner of the year with a record amount of $65,819.81. (Photo by courtesy of MacGregor, Cincinnati, Ohio)

"When the Great Scorer comes, to mark against your name,
He'll write not won or lost, but how you played the game."
The name of Grantland Rice is known to every lover of
sports. He was the Dean of all Sportswriters and the leading
authority in America. In 1939 he suggested the Hall of Fame,
which was instituted and is now quite successful. In 1954,
Granny finally wrote his great book, *The Tumult and the
Shouting*, A.S. Barnes & Co., which was a most remarkable
treatise of himself and sports. Shortly after. he bid us all a
farewell. No one yet has taken his place. (Photo by courtesy
of David Scott Chisholm)

Samuel Jackson Snead captured his third Master's title in 1954 when he defeated Ben Hogan in one of the most thrilling playoffs in the game. Hogan hit every green in regulation figures, while Snead missed five, yet Snead won by a single stroke. Hogan three putted only on the 16th green while Snead putted most brilliantly to win. (Photo by courtesy of Wilson Sporting Goods, Chicago, Ill.)

Ellsworth Vines is one of the rare two-sport athletes in recent history. He was the world's leading amateur tennis player of the 1930's then became a golf professional in 1942. Pro golf highlights include the runner-up spot in the All-American Open in 1946, semifinalist in the P.G.A. Championship of 1951, and winner of the California Open in 1954. (Photo by courtesy of Wilson Sporting Goods, Chicago, Ill.)

Jack Fleck, the surprise winner of the U.S. Open Championship in 1955. Although considered a "black-sheep" winner, Jack did it the hard way; he defeated the great Ben Hogan in a playoff. It appeared that Hogan had won his fifth Open, but Jack birdied two of the last four holes to tie, then won the playoff. (Photo by courtesy of Spalding, Mass.)

play. There were 45,000 spectators attending this first stroke play event who paid a record of over $95,000 in gate receipts.

The number of golf courses in the U.S. reached a total of 5700. Strangely enough, this is the same number which existed in 1931. With the Depression forcing many courses and clubs to close, plus World War II effects, it took this long to regain this number of courses.[118]

The first World Amateur Golf Team Championship was played in 1958 over the famed Royal and Ancient course at St. Andrews, Scotland. Representatives from 29 countries competed for the Eisenhower Trophy and the country of Australia was victorious.[119]

In 1959 the professional golfers of the U.S. played for a total of $1,109,755 in 43 PGA co-sponsored tournaments which marked the first time the one million dollar mark was exceeded.[120] During the same year, over four million Americans

A smiling Dr. Cary Middlecoff who won his second U.S. Open Championship in 1956. In the year before, 1955, Cary also won the Masters Tournament by a record margin of seven strokes. He scorched the course in the second round with a 65 and finished with a 279 total, seven strokes in front of Ben Hogan. (Photo by courtesy of Wilson Sporting Goods, Chicago, Ill.)

Ted Kroll, four times wounded in World War II, achieved considerable fame in 1956, by winning the world's championship, the Tucson and Houston Opens, and ended the year as the leading money winner. Ted has played on three U.S. Ryder Cup teams. Although Ted turned professional in 1937, he did not begin to play regularly on the tour until 1950. (Photo by courtesy of MacGregor, Cincinnati, Ohio)

Ted Kroll

Jack Burke, Jr., added the National PGA Championship to his credit in 1956 at the Blue Hills Country Club, Mass., where he defeated Ted Kroll in the finals. Earlier in the year, Jack had won the Masters Tournament which gave him two major titles in the same year. (Photo by courtesy of MacGregor, Cincinnati, Ohio)

On the practice tee at the Áugusta National Golf Course prior to the Masters Tournament of 1966. (Photo by Nevin H. Gibson)

Lionel Hebert

Richard Sikes

Mike Souchak

Ben Hogan

A shot of the 18th green of the Olympic Golf Club, San Francisco, during the 1966 National Open Championship. At this time, Ben Hogan is making his last putt for a 70, while Arnold Palmer and Billy Casper are just starting on the back nine, with Palmer in the lead by seven strokes. As recorded, Casper gained the deficit and won the playoff the following day, again coming from behind.

A view of the eighth green of the Olympic Golf Course during the National Open Championship in 1966. (Photo by Nevin H. Gibson)

The aftermath of a tournament. Beyond the litter, the scoreboard reads Palmer — Casper two under at 278. Playoff tomorrow. (Photos by Nevin H. Gibson)

A view of the entire 18th hole of the Olympic Golf Club during the final round of the National Open Championship of 1966, as seen from the clubhouse. (Photo by Nevin H. Gibson)

Doug Ford, one of the fastest players in the game, added the Masters Tournament to his credit in 1957. A few weeks prior to the Masters, Ford predicted he would win with a 283 to *Golf World* Magazine at the National Golf Show in N.Y. He did precisely that when he holed out a sand trap shot on the last green for his 283. Previously, Ford won the National PGA Championship in 1955 at Meadowbrook, C.C., Michigan, where he defeated Cary Middlecoff in the final round by 4 & 3. Ford, a native of New York, has been one of the leading money winners on the tour. (Photo by courtesy of MacGregor, Cincinnati, Ohio)

Miss Heidi, two years old, with her most capable caddy at the 1957 National Golf Show in N.Y. This scene from the National Guard Armory shows an authentic live green which was transplanted inside the building for this one week show. A putting contest and a "hole in one" tournament were held therein. (Photo by Meljay, by courtesy of Lillian Harlow, *Golf World* Magazine)

Mr. Jack Level, owner of the world's largest collection of golf oddities, exhibits one dozen old featheries — the golf balls which were used for centuries up to 1848, before the introduction of gutta-percha. In 1902, Dr. Haskell's rubber-cored ball replaced the "gutties.!" (Photo by Robert T. Olsen by courtesy of Jack Level)

The colorful Paul Hahn, currently the greatest "trick shot" artist in the game. Paul has been all over the world to demonstrate his variety of golf magic. He flys his own plane and is in great demand. (Photo by courtesy of Paul Hahn)

played at least ten times or more and a total of 81,250,000 rounds was played. The televising of golf tournaments and President Eisenhower's enthusiasm for the game are major contributing factors to golf's rapid expansion in the U.S. and abroad. In 1960 a record total of 6,011 golf courses was in existence in the U.S. A breakdown on the type of courses follow:

	9 Hole Courses	18 Hole Courses	Total
Private Courses	1,607	1,555	3,162
Semi-Private Courses	1,371	625	1,997
Municipal Courses	406	446	852
Totals	3,385	2,626	6,011[121]

During the same year, 1960, Arnold Palmer became the PGA Player of the year and showed marks of immortality by winning the Masters Tournament, the U.S. Open Championship, Best Performance Average, and was the leading money winner for a record of $75,262.[122]

In 1961 the Professional Golfers Association set a prize record of $1,492,200 in 45 tournaments. Gary Player, from South Africa, became the first foreigner to win the leading share for $64,540.[123]

Golf continued to make tremendous strides in 1962 in the aspect of equipment sold and the number or persons playing the game. The televising of golf matches and tournaments exceeded all other sports with the exception of baseball. The immortal

Miss Patty Berg who in 1958 won her seventh Women's Western Open Championship at Erie, Pa., for a record number of victories. Patty also holds seven Women's Titleholders Championships and she was the first winner of the U.S. Women's Championship in 1946, which was held in Spokane, Washington. (Photo by courtesy of Wilson Sporting Goods, Chicago, Ill.)

"Thundering" Tommy Bolt, so noted for his club-throwing ability, gives a small demonstration here when his birdie putt circled the hole, then failed to drop. Tommy won the U.S. National Open title in 1958 at Tulsa, Okla. He is one of the best dressers in the game and maintains a huge wardrobe which accompanies him on tour. (Photo by courtesy of Bruce Koch, Rochester, N.Y.)

Ben Hogan showing his old form. He hits shot from second fairway at the Masters Golf Tournament in 1960 during second round to score a 68. The little Texan ended in sixth place. Not bad for a retired professional. (Photo by courtesy of Bruce Koch, Rochester, N.Y.)

Miss Barbara McIntire at the Congressional Country Club, Wash., D.C., with the U.S. Women's Amateur trophy which she won thereat in 1959. Barbara defeated Miss Joanne Goodwin in the final round by 4 & 3. (Photo by courtesy of Vince Finnigan, Wash., D.C.)

Art Wall, Jr., the 1959 Masters Tournament winner. Among other things Art won in 1959 were the Vardon Trophy, the PGA Player of the Year, Leading Money Winner, and three other championships. Art holds the world's record for the number of holes in one. The last count was 38. This lean Pennsylvanian is a Duke graduate and turned pro in 1949. (Photo by courtesy of Wilson Sporting Goods, Chicago, Ill.)

The present and past winners of the Masters Tournament in 1960. (Seated from left): Horton Smith, Gene Sarazen, Jimmy Demaret, Sam Snead, Bob Jones, Art Wall, Clifford Roberts, Claude Harmon, Doug Ford, Arnold Palmer. (Standing): Jack Burke, Henry Picard, Craig Wood, Cary Middlecoff, Byron Nelson, Herman Keiser, Ben Hogan. Ralph Guldahl is missing. The winner in 1960 was Arnold Palmer. (Photo by Morgan Fitz)

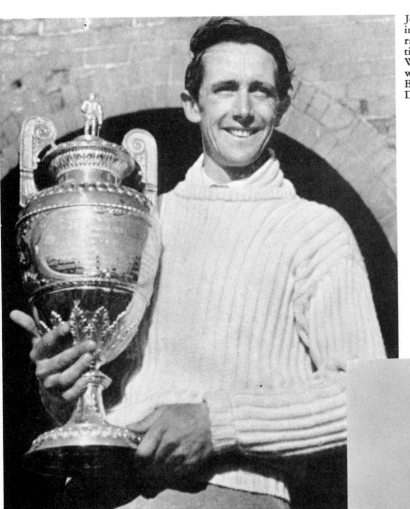

Joseph B. Carr, winner of the British Amateur Championship in 1960 at The Royal Portrush where he defeated Bob Cochran in the final round by 7 and 6. It was the third Amateur title for Carr. In his first victory, in 1953, he defeated Harvie Ward of the U.S. in the finals at Hoylake. His second victory was in 1958 at St. Andrews, Scotland. Carr has played on the British Walker Cup team since 1947. (Photo by courtesy of D. M. Mathieson, *Golfer's Handbook,* Great Britain)

Jay Hebert, winner of the U.S. Professional Golfers Championship at the Firestone Country Club at Akron, Ohio, in 1960. Jay's brother, Lionel, won the same event in 1955. (Photo by Spalding Company, Mass.)

Betsy Rawls and the swing which helped her win a record of four U.S. Women's Open Championships. Betsy, a graduate of the University of Texas, won her fourth title at Worcester Country Club, Mass., in 1960. (Photo by Wilson Sporting Goods Company)

"Little" Jerry Barber (5' 5", 135 pounds) was the smallest to win the National PGA Championship. Jerry won in a playoff against Don January when he sank a 60-foot putt on the last green at Olympia Fields C.C., Ill., in 1961. Jerry, at age forty-five, was also the oldest to win. (Photo by Spalding)

Arnold Palmer won the Masters Tournament and successfully defended his British Open title. He ended the year as the leading money winner with $81,448 in official winnings, which established a new record. Golf also continued to lead in the sales of sporting goods.[124]

As of February 1963, the value of golf facilities in the U.S. was estimated at $1,556,000,000. Of the estimated 6,000,000 golfers in the U.S., 700,-000 are women.[125] The Pro-etts competed for over $300,000. The men professionals also competed for a record amount of $2,044,900 in prize money. It was in 1959, when the men professionals competed for over one million dollars for a record.

This in itself gives us some conception of golf's growing popularity during this short period. By the end of 1963 there were 7419 golf courses in the U.S.[126]

In 1964, there were over 9,000,000 Americans playing on 8500 golf courses in the United States. Also, a total of $128,254,462. was spent on golf equipment.[127] During the following year, Americans spent $139,998,552. for golf clubs, balls, bags, and other items, excluding golf carts.[128]

Arnold Palmer's 1964 Masters victory gave him an unprecedented four Masters Championships. In six of the last seven Masters Tournaments, he has been third place or better. This major championship

Bob Goalby, the handsome professional from Illinois, was tied with Doug Sanders for runner-up spot in the U.S. Open Championship in 1961. Later, Bob set a record by scoring eight consecutive birdies in a PGA event which has yet to be broken. (Photo by courtesy of Spalding Co., Mass.)

Mr. Joseph C. Dey, Jr., Executive Director of the United States Golf Association since 1935. One of the most knowledgeable men on golf, he directs the vast mechanism which makes this world's largest golfing fraternity function. He has indeed served most admirably. His words, although quietly spoken, are unimpeachable. He is without refute — *Mr. Golf*. (Photo by the United States Golf Association)

Jack Nicklaus with wife Barbara at New Orleans where he won the Western Amateur Championship in 1961. Jack turned pro the following year. (Photo by courtesy of the Western Golf Association)

172

Sam Snead, runner-up, is congratulating Arnold Palmer, the winner of the Western Open championship, of 1961 at Blythefield C.C., Grand Rapids, Mich. (Photo by Western Golf Association)

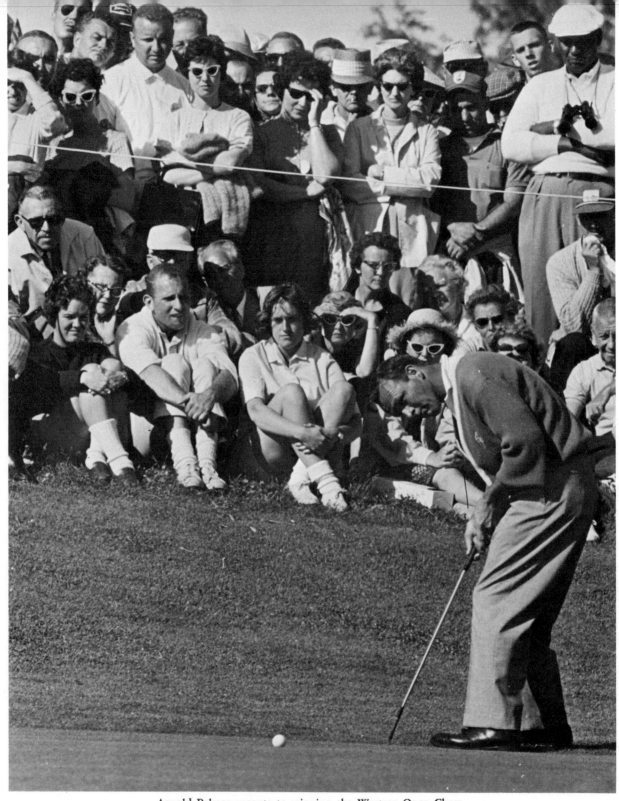

Arnold Palmer enroute to winning the Western Open Championship at the Blythefield C.C. in Grand Rapids, Mich., in 1961. (Photo by Western Golf Association)

Arnold Palmer playing an exhibition match at Warrington, Va., for the United States Air Force. He played the new difficult 7000 yard layout in most brilliant fashion, sight unseen. Notice his powerful arms in this photo which account for his tremendous drives and compels his army to utter the "ohs" on every tee shot. (Photo by courtesy of the United States Air Force, Wash., D.C.)

Marilynn Smith added the Women's Titleholders Championship to her credit in 1963. One of the top women professionals, Marilynn is a great favorite with the gallery. (Photo by courtesy of Spalding, Mass.)

gives the immortal golfer a total of seven major titles, the same record possessed by Gene Sarazen and Sam Snead. During the same year, Ken Venturi, in perhaps one of the greatest comebacks in sporting history, won the U.S. Open Championship at the Congressional C.C., in Washington, D.C. Ken, according to his own admission, was all washed up as a golf-touring professional. However, with the aid of salt tablets and with tremendous faith, he came through wih a blazing finish which equaled the terrific heat wave which prevailed at the time for his greatest victory. He also added the Insurance City Open and the American Golf Classic to his credit before the year ended.[129] On the feminine side, Mickey Wright, the immortal woman professional, scored her most exciting year. Through illness and the burden of the LPGA presidency in 1963 and 1964, plus the strain of retaining her "status-quo," she emerged victorious in the U.S. Woman's Open Championship for a record tying four wins. She also became the leading money winner for the fourth consecutive time and her total of

Arnold Palmer in his renown putting stance sinking a six-footer in an exhibition match at Warrington, Va. (Photo by courtesy of the United States Air Force, Washington, D.C.)

Willie Hunter and son, Mac, descendants from the famed golf Scottish clan. Willie's father, Harry, was the professional at the Royal Cinque Ports G.C., Deal, England, for 46 years. Willie himself has been at the Riviera C.C., Los Angeles, for over 30 years, and is now the pro-Emeritus. His son, Mac, is now head pro. Mac won the National Junior Championship at Oakland Hills and defeated none other than Arnold Palmer in the finals. He is probably the most brilliant golf pro merchandizer in the business. (Photo by Jimmy Dale, by courtesy of Willie Hunter)

Dave Ragan, the touring professional from Florida, was the runner-up to Jack Nicklaus in the National PGA Championship in Dallas in 1963. (Photo by courtesy Spalding, Mass.)

Miss Mickey Wright, the all time leading money winner in the feminine ranks. Mickey has broken practically every record in the books and is still the leading contender in every tournament she enters. She hails from Texas. (Photo by courtesy of Wilson Sporting Goods, Chicago, Ill.)

11 tournament victories gave her the Woman's Tournament Champion Award. Mickey also won the Vare Trophy for the fifth consecutive time which is a record that has never been approached. The professional women played in 32 tournaments this year for a total purse of $330,000. The men professionals played in 41 tournaments which paid $2,301,063. in official prize money.[130]

In 1965 there were 8332 golf courses in existence in the U.S., including 881 par three's. The total amount of "active" golfers is 7,750,000. There are probably 10 million all told who play at least once a year.[131] Big Jack Nicklaus captured his second Masters victory this year with the finest performance in the history of the tournament with a record score of 271. He won by 11 strokes over his friendly rivals, Arnold Palmer and Gary Player. These three are referred to as the "big three." Jack also ended the year as the leading money winner with a record of $140,752. Gary Player of South Africa became the first outsider to win the U.S. Open Championship. He also became the third golfer to win all

The most venerable Sam Snead who in 1965 won the Greater Greensboro Open for a record ninth time. Sam, possessor of the smoothest swing in golf, has been on tour for over 30 years and he is still going strong. His record is most brilliant. To name some of his laurels: winner, British Open; three-time winner of the Nat'l PGA Championship; three-time leading money winner; four-time winner of the Vardon Trophy; nine-time member of the Ryder Cup Team; winner of the World's Senior Championship; and Member of the Golf Hall of Fame. (Photo by courtesy of Wilson Sporting Goods Co., Chicago, Ill.)

"Champagne" Tony Lema after winning the British Open Championship in 1964 over the famed Royal & Ancient Golf Club of St. Andrews, Scotland. He purchased the champagne for the press and thus endowed the name. (Photo by Dick Taylor, *Golf World Magazine*)

Bruce Devlin of Armidale, Australia, has made several successful bids for top golf titles in the U.S., and has been successful also in the money winning department. In 1965 he won $67,657.78 and in 1966 he collected $49,145.16. In 1966 he won both the Colonial National and the Carling World Open. (Photo by courtesy Spalding Co.)

Gary Player from South Africa, but an International favorite
the world over, has won every major championship under
the sun. He won the three leading championships of the
United States and is the only outsider to ever come close.
In 1961 he was also the leading money winner in the U.S.,
the first foreigner to accomplish this feat. (Photo by courtesy
of Bruce Koch, Rochester, N.Y.)

"AND AWAY WE GO"
(1965)   Jackie Gleason driving, with Arnold Palmer, during
the Jackie Gleason Pro-Amateur Tournament at Doral Golf
Club, Miami, Fla. (Photo by courtesy of the Doral Golf Club
and Hotel, Miami, Fla.)

One of the most picturesque golf courses in the world, Pebbie Beach. This is the famed 18th hole. (Photo by courtesy of Bing Crosby. By Julian P. Graham Photo)

A characteristic expression of Arnold Palmer, accommodating the youths with his autograph. (Photo by courtesy of Western Golf ASS.)

185

Billy Casper won the 1966 U.S. Open Championship the most impossible way. He was seven strokes back of Arnold Palmer with nine holes to go and he tied Arnie on the last hole. He shot two under while Arnie went five over. Then Casper won the playoff. (Photo by courtesy of Wilson Sporting Goods, Chicago, Ill.)

four of the major championships and therefore joins Gene Sarazen and Ben Hogan with this distinction. In 1961 Gary was also the first foreigner to become the leading money winner in PGA official earnings. Across the Atlantic, Peter Thomson topped a rugged field of competitors, including the immortals from the U.S., to win his fifth British Open Championship. Only Harry Vardon, with six victories, has more. The U.S. Amateur Championship changed to stroke play in lieu of match play for the first time and Bob Murphy of Florida, an unknown, was victorious. He was the second amateur in history to win in his first try. England's Harold H. Hilton did it in 1911.[132] However, Hilton was already an immortal amateur in Great Britain at the time. On the basis of manufacturers' selling prices, golf equipment sales in 1965 totaled $139,998,552 — 9.3 percent over 1964's total of $128,249,046.[133]

In 1966 Jack Nicklaus became the first golfer to successfully defend a Masters title which gave him

Waiting to tee off at Cypress Point during the 25th Annual
Crosby Pro-Amateur. Left to right: Tony Lema, Father John
Durkin, and Billy Casper. The Crosby Clambake affair is
growing in popularity every year. Here the top professionals
are paired off with noted amateurs who play by handicaps.
These celebrated amateurs plus national TV coverage have
tremendously added to the Crosby clambake. (Photo by
courtesy of Bing Crosby. By Julian P. Graham)

Jack Nicklaus, the world's most sensational golfer during the past five years, is seen finishing a drive. Jack is the longest hitter in the game. Jack has won every major championship and is striving to become the world's greatest golfer. (Watch out Arnie) (Photo by courtesy of Bruce Koch, N.Y.)

Clive Clark of Great Britain is shown about to drop 35-foot putt on final green in final match to halve Mark Hopkins of U.S., and give Britain an 11-11 tie — the first in history of Walker Cup Matches — at Five Farms Course of Baltimore C.C., Sept. 4, 1965. The British were on the verge of losing their 10th straight Walker Cup competition after holding a 10-5 edge before the final eight singles matches. The Americans won six of the eight final-day singles matches, lost one, and tied one for the biggest comeback in Walker Cup history. The British have won only one of the 20 Walker Cup matches, 7-4, at St Andrews in 1938. (Photo by Joe Gambatese, *Golf Guide*)

Deane Beman of Bethesda, Md., holes 12-foot putt on 18th green to defeat Sandy Saddler of Great Britain, 1 up, and keep alive U.S. chances of winning in Walker Cup matches at Baltimore C.C.'s Five Farms Course, Sept. 4, 1965. If Beman had missed, the U.S. could have done no better than tie. (Photo by Joe Gambatese, *Golf Guide*)

Allen L. Geiberger and wife Judy with $25,000 check and trophy, after winning the National PGA Championship in 1966 at the Firestone C.C., in Akron, Ohio. (Photo by courtesy of the Firestone C.C., Akron, Ohio)

a total of three. Jack also won the British Open Championship which gives this youthful professional a total of six major victories (not including two U.S. Amateurs), and each of the four major professional titles. He therefore becomes the fourth professional to win all four. Within a short period of five years, "Big" Jack has amassed one of the greatest professional records in the history of the game. He is second only to Arnold Palmer in all-time money winnings. Again the prize money rose to another record purse. In 36 official events, $3,-117,780 was presented in prize money which topped the 1965 prize by $257,515.[134] Furthermore, approximately one million dollars in prize money was added to the unofficial PGA events, such as the Carling World Championship, the Crosby, Hope, and the World Championship of Golf, just to name a few. The biggest surprise in 1966 took place at the Olympic Club in San Francisco, the venue for the U.S. Open Championship. During the final round, Palmer, playing with Billy Casper, was seven strokes in the lead at the end of nine holes. At this precise point, the infallible Ben Hogan had just made his last putt on the 18th green for a most respectable 70 and his followers joined "Arnie's Army." Through the remaining nine holes, Casper gained stroke after stroke and eventually ended in a tie on the last hole. In the playoff, Arnie took a two-stroke lead but Casper also gained this

prize after winning over the team of Sanders and Besselink by three strokes. Two-man teams (best-ball), comprising 320 professionals competed in this affair. By the end of the year, $4,144,991.59 was paid in prizes which included the unofficial events. Billy Casper received the largest share for $121,944. This made Billy the second all-time

Deane R. Beman, left, twice U.S. National Amateur winner (1960 and 1963), and the British Amateur king in 1959, presents the author, Nevin H. Gibson, with a small golf trophy which he won in local tournament in Washington, D.C. Deane turned professional in 1967 after a most successful venture in the amateur ranks. (Photo by courtesy of George Arble, Wash., D.C.)

deficit and finally won by four strokes. Apart from Francis Ouimet's Open victory in 1913, it marked the biggest surprise in the history of the U.S. Open Championship. It also marked the third time that Palmer lost in a playoff for the U.S. Open Championship.[135]

The Professional Golfers Association sponsored a PGA National Team Championship which awarded a purse of $275,000.00 which was the largest single purse ever established for a golf tournament. This event was held on their own PGA National Golf Club course at Palm Beach Gardens, Florida in December of 1966. Arnold Palmer, teamed with Jack Nicklaus, split the $50,000 first

money winner in official PGA events with $593,942 in earnings. Arnold Palmer leads with $755,401.-00.[136] There was approximately a 15 per cent decline in the number of golf courses constructed in 1966 in comparison with the previous year. This was due to the "tight" mortgage lenders and is a temporary situation. As the year ended there were some 8,672 golf courses in play in the U.S., which include 943 par three's. An estimated 176,000,000 rounds of golf were played in 1966.[137]

Favorite courses feature a psychological advantage as proven by Al Gieberger in winning the Golden Anniversary National PGA Championship at the Firestone C.C., in Akron, Ohio. He had

Putting methods and strokes of some professionals who participated in the $100,000 Doral Open Championship in March of 1967, at Miami, Florida. Doug Sanders was the winner. (Photo by Nevin H. Gibson)

Juan "Chi Chi" Rodriguez

Dave Marr

"Big" George Bayer

Dow Finsterwald

Two veterans in the field of professional golf, Jimmy Demaret and Gene Sarazen. In days bygone these professionals have won ten major championships and countless other events. They are now connected with golf but in the television division. They comment and assist in the filming of *Shell's Wonderful World of Golf*, a successful TV program which selects courses all over the world then has the top professionals compete in matches. (Photo by courtesy of Shell's Wonderful World of Golf)

1965 — Mary Barrow proudly holds the trophies and wears the traditional blazer awarded her for winning the Fourth Annual Military Dependents Golf Championship at Andrews Air Force Base, Maryland. Mrs. Eugene Zuckert, wife of the Secretary of the Air Force and honorary chairman of the event, made the presentation. (Photo by courtesy of the United States Air Force, Wash., D.C.)

The venerable Sam Snead changes his putting stroke after 35 years. Sam had the putting yips so bad in the National PGA event in 1966 at Akron that he changed to this method for short putts. He has successfully used this same method ever since. (Photo by courtesy of the Firestone C.C., Akron, Ohio)

This was perhaps the very last photograph taken of Tony Lema. It was during the National PGA Championship at Akron, Ohio, in 1966. Shortly afterwards, Tony and his lovely wife were killed in an airplane crash enroute to his next golf event. "Champagne" Tony was loved by all — the press, spectators, and his fellow pros. (Photo by courtesy of the Firestone C.C., Akron, Ohio)

The big leaders of the Professional Golfers Association of America. L to R: Max Elbin, president; Warren Orlick, treasurer; and Leo Fraser, secretary. The executive director (not shown) is Robert T. Greasey. (Photo courtesy of Pro., Golfers Asso. of Am.)

Gene Littler hugging the World Series of Golf Championship Trophy he won in 1966. Four contestants compete for this award annually, which are the winners of the four major championships: The U.S. Open, the British Open, the Masters, and the National PGA Championship. (Photo by courtesy of the Firestone C.C., Akron, Ohio)

The score placard alone is sufficient caption for this photograph. (Photo by courtesy of Firestone C.C., Akron, Ohio)

195

The immortal Arnold Palmer, the all-time leading money winner of the world, with his jet airplane. The youthful multi-millionaire has made an indelible mark in the history of golf in such a relative short period — actually, since 1958. He is still going strong and is the one to beat in each event. (Photo by courtesy of Arnold Palmer)

previously won the American Golf Classic at the Firestone Club in 1965 with an identical score of 280 and in both events his margin of victory was four strokes. Immediately after the PGA Championship, tragedy struck as Tony Lema and his wife, Betty, died in a private plane crash. The Lemas were being flown to Lansing, Ill., where he was to compete in a one-day tournament. The pilot and co-pilot also died in the crash.[138]

Deane Beman, one of the outstanding amateurs of the world, was on the brink of winning his third U.S. Amateur title but blew the last two holes and tied Gary Cowan of Canada at 285. Gary won the playoff. Later, Deane announced his decision to become a professional. He departs the amateur field with two U.S. Amateur titles, one British Amateur, and a number of semi-major titles.[139]

In the first major tournament of 1967, "Big"

A complete followthrough by Jack Nicklaus, the longest hitter in the game. Millions have yearned to learn the secret of his power, also, his fellow professionals. It is however known that he swings very hard and *all the way,* as indicated in this photo. (Photo by courtesy of Bruce Koch, Rochester, N.Y.)

Doug Sanders enroute to winning the Doral $100,000 Open at Miami, Florida, March 5, 1967. It was the Sixth Annual Doral Open held at the fabulous Doral Country Club and Hotel.

198

Putting styles of four professionals who have won major championships. Taken at the 1967 $100,000 Doral Open Championship. Gay Brewer won the Masters Tournament just after this event. (Photos by Nevin H. Gibson)

Bobby Nichols — PGA Champion of 1964

Lionel Hebert — PGA Champion of 1957

Gay Brewer — Masters Champion of 1967

Jack Fleck — U.S. Open Champion of 1955

Tom Weiskopf (left) and Mason Rudolph are teammates in the 1967 CBS Golf Classic at the Firestone Country Club, Akron, Ohio, the venue for this tournament and the World Series of Golf. (Photo by courtesy of the Firestone C.C., Akron, Ohio)

Jack Nicklaus surprised the golfing world when he failed to qualify for the final 36 holes in the Masters Tournament at the Augusta National Golf Club. Jack had won three Master titles previously, including the last two in succession; therefore, he was most desirous to make it three in a row. Under these circumstances his failure to make the cut was indeed a low blow to himself which precluded his chances of seeking an unprecedented record. On the final day of play, Gay Brewer fired an excellent score of 67 to win a most deserving victory by a single stroke. In the previous year, and in the presence of some 5,000,000 television spectators, Gay had only a short putt to make on the final hole in order to win this most "prestigeous" event, but the ball remained on the left side of the hole "looking in" but it failed to drop. Thus, instant fame had escaped Gay Brewer. But opportunity knocked again this year and Gay responded to the call most courageously to win his first major championship.[140]

Putting strokes and methods of some professionals who participated in the $100,000 Doral Open Championship in March of 1967, at Miami, Florida. Doug Sanders was the winner. Art Wall, Jr., was the runner-up. (Photos by Nevin H. Gibson)

Jack Nicklaus

Bruce Devlin

Doug Sanders

Art Wall, Jr.

Also in 1967, Roberto De Vicenzo, the international touring professional from Argentina, won the British Open Championship after trying in this event twenty times. His 278 total edged Jack Nicklaus by two strokes. Roberto has won more national championships than all other professionals and his British Open victory at Hoylake was his first major title. The final two rounds were televised live to the U.S. via Satellite.

"Big" Jack Nicklaus established a record 275 to win the 67th U.S. National Open Championship at Baltusrol, N.J. At age twenty-seven, Nicklaus has made a staggering record. In five of the last eight Opens he has won twice and finished among the first four. He has won the British Open, the National PGA of America, the United States Amateur twice, the Masters thrice, and has shared in three Canada Cup victories over the professionals around the world. His scoring feats have been phenomenal. Besides his 275 in the Open, there stand out his four great rounds at Merion in the 1960 World Amateur Team Championships: 66–67–68–68 — 269, over one of the classic courses — perhaps the four best rounds ever played in one tournament. In the 1965 Masters at Augusta National he set a record of 67–71–64–69 — 271. Nicklaus must surely be recognized as the Complete Golfer.[141] Nicklaus has now won a total of nine major championships, seven of these in the professional field.

Two Dons from Texas, January and Massengale, vied for the 1967 National PGA title and January was victorious after a playoff at the Columbine, C.C., in Denver, Colorado. January lost this same event in a playoff with Jerry Barber in 1961. His victory in Denver was most deserving and his playoff score of 69 against Masengale's 71 presented an excellent show for a record number of over 10,000 spectators.

For the first time in the history of the U.S. Woman's Open Championship an Amateur won the title in 1967 at the Homestead Golf Club in Hot Springs, Virginia. Catherine Lacoste of Paris, France, not only became the first Amateur to win but the first foreign champion as well. The new champion — also holder of the French Amateur title — comes by her athletic talent hereditarily. Her father, millionaire Rene Lacoste, is past holder of the Wimbledon and U.S. tennis titles and mother, the former Mlle. Thion de la Chaume, won the 1927 British Ladies Amateur and was a quarterfinalist in the U.S. Amateur the same year. Ironically, her mother was the first outsider to win the British Ladies Championship.[142] Written of Catherine's mother, 40 years ago: "Mademoiselle Simone Thion de la Chaume has made a niche for herself in the history of ladies' golf. To her has fallen the great distinction of being the first overseas competitor to win the British Ladies' Championship since the event was instituted in 1893."[143]

Appendix

PAST RECORDS

AMATEUR LEADERS TO 1885

	Total Points	Royal Medal	Silver Cross	Gold Medal	Silver Medal	Average Score
W. H. M. Dougall	21	3	2	3	5	97.7
L. M. Balfour	20	4	0	4	4	91.2
J. O. Fairlie	14	2	3	0	2	99.1
Robert Clark	12	1	3	1	2	94.5
W. C. Thomson	12	1	3	1	2	97.0
Alex. Stuart	11	2	2	1	0	88.2
Charles Anderson	11	2	1	1	2	91.5
Thomas Hodge	11	3	0	0	2	93.6
G. M. Innes	9	1	2	0	2	97.0
Robert Hay	9	2	1	1	0	101.0

Computation of Points: Royal Medal, 3 points; Silver Medal, 2; Gold Medal, 1; Silver Medal, 1. All events held at the R. & A. G. C., St. Andrews. Royal Medal, 1st prize of Autumn meeting; Silver Cross, 2nd prize. Gold Medal, 1st prize of Spring meeting; Silver Medal, 2nd prize.

PROFESSIONAL LEADERS TO 1885

	Total Points	British Open Titles	Runner-up	Average Winning Score	Average No. of Entrants
Tom Morris	16	4	4	165.75	11
Willie Park	16	4	4	169.25	13
Tom Morris, Jr.	12	4		156.50	13
Jamie Anderson	10	3	1	162.33	25
Bob Ferguson	10	3	1	167.67	40
Bob Martin	7	2	1	173.50	42
Willie Fernie	5	1	2	159.00	11
Andrew Strath	4	1	1	162.00	10

Total points computed by awarding three points for each British Open winner and one point for each runner-up. These statistics are based on the Professional's performance in the British Open from 1860 1885.

ALL-TIME LEADERS TO 1918

	TOTAL POINTS	TOTAL MAJORS WON	OPEN EVENTS MAJORS					OPEN EVENTS S-MAJORS					AMATEUR EVENTS MAJORS				AMATEUR EVENTS S-MAJORS				
PROFESSIONALS			BRITISH OPEN	R/U BRITISH OPEN	U.S. NATIONAL OPEN	R/U NATIONAL OPEN	NEWS OF THE WORLD G/B	FRENCH OPEN	BELGIAN OPEN	U.S. WESTERN OPEN	METROPOLITAN OPEN	NORTH & SOUTH OPEN	BRITISH AMATEUR	R/U BRITISH AMATEUR	U.S. AMATEUR	R/U U.S. AMATEUR	FRENCH (O) AMATEUR	WESTERN AMATEUR U.S.	METROPOLITAN AMATEUR	NORTH & SOUTH AMATEUR	IRISH (O) AMATEUR
1 – Harry Vardon	27	7	6	4	1	1	1														
2 – John H. Taylor	26	5	5	6		1	2	2													
3 – James Braid	23	5	5	3			4	1													
4 – Willie Anderson	16	4			4	1				3											
5 – Alexander Smith	15	2			2	3				2	4										
6 – Arnaud Massy	8	1	1	1				3	1												
7 – John J. McDermott	8	2			2	1				1											
8 – Alexander Ross	8	1			1							5									
9 – Alexander Herd	7	1	1	3				1													
10 – Tom McNamara	7	0				3				1	1	2									
AMATEURS																					
1 – John Ball	34	9	1	1									8	3							3
2 – Harold H. Hilton	26	7	2										4	3	1						4
3 – Jerome D. Travers	21	5			1										4	1		5			
4 – Walter J. Travis	20	4				1							1		3				4	3	
5 – Charles Evans Jr.	15	2			1	1				1					1	1	1	4		1	
6 – H. Chandler Egan	11	2													2	1		4			
7 – John E. Laidlay	10	2	1										2	3							
8 – H. G. Hutchinson	8	2											2	2							
9 – Francis Ouimet	8	2			1										1		1	4			
10 – Findley S. Douglas	7	1													1	2			2		
11 – Robert A. Gardner	7	2													2	1					

COMPUTATION OF POINTS

3 points for each Major tournament victory.
1 point for each Major tournament runner-up.
1 point for each Semi-major tournament victory.

The chart shows the specific Semi-majors and Majors each leader won during this period.

	TOTAL POINTS	TOTAL MAJORS WON	NATIONAL OPEN	R/U NATIONAL OPEN	BRITISH OPEN	R/U BRITISH OPEN	U.S. PROFESSIONALS G/C	R/U U.S. PROFESSIONALS	MASTERS TOURNAMENT	WESTERN OPEN	METROPOLITAN OPEN	NORTH & SOUTH OPEN	CANADIAN OPEN	FRENCH OPEN	BRITISH AMATEUR	R/U BRITISH AMATEUR	NATIONAL AMATEUR	R/U NATIONAL AMATEUR	WESTERN AMATEUR	METROPOLITAN AMATEUR	NORTH & SOUTH AMATEUR	SOUTHERN AMATEUR	CANADIAN AMATEUR
PROFESSIONALS																							
1 – Walter Hagen	49	11	2	1	4	1	5	1		5	3	3	1	1									
2 – Gene Sarazen	26	7	2	1	1	1	3	1	1	1	1												
3 – James Barnes	19	4	1		1	1	2	2		3		1											
4 – Tommy D. Armour	15	3	1		1		1	1		1	1	3	3										
5 – Leo Diegel	13	2		1		1	2	1					4										
6 – Macdonald Smith	12	0		2		2				3	3		1										
7 – Jock Hutchinson	11	2		1	1		1	1		2		1											
8 – Olin Dutra	7	2	1				1				1												
9 – Johnny Farrell	6	1	1			1		1			1												
10 – Willie MacFarlane	5	1	1								2												
AMATEURS																							
1 – Robert T. Jones	48	13	4	4	3										1		5	2				3	
2 – Charles Evans	24	3	1	1						1				1			2	3	8		1		
3 – Francis Ouimet	13	3	1											1			2	1	1				
4 – Lawson Little	12	4													2		2						
5 – Robert A. Gardner	9	2														1	2	2					
6 – Jess W. Sweetser	8	2													1		1	1		1			
7 – C. R. Somerville	8	1															1						5
8 – George T. Dunlap	7	1															1					4	
9 – Johnny Goodman	4	1	1															1					
10 – George Von Elm (P-31)	4	1		1													1	1					

COMPUTATION OF POINTS

3 points for each Major tournament victory.
1 point   for each Semi-major tournament victory.
1 point   for each Major tournament runner-up.

The chart shows the specific Semi-majors and Majors each leader won during this period.

PROFESSIONALS	TOTAL POINTS	TOTAL MAJORS WON	NATIONAL OPEN	R/U NATIONAL OPEN	BRITISH OPEN	R/U BRITISH OPEN	MASTERS	R/U MASTERS	U.S. PGA	R/U U.S. PGA	WESTERN OPEN	CANADIAN OPEN	WORLDS CHAMPION	METROPOLITAN OPEN	NORTH & SOUTH OPEN	NATIONAL AMATEUR	R/U NATIONAL AMATEUR	BRITISH AMATEUR	R/U BRITISH AMATEUR	WESTERN AMATEUR	NORTH & SOUTH AMATEUR	METROPOLITAN AMATEUR	CANADIAN AMATEUR	PACIFIC NORTHWEST AMATEUR	TRANS-MISSISSIPPI AMATEUR	FRENCH OPEN AMATEUR
			MAJORS								S-MAJORS					MAJORS				S-MAJORS						
1 – Ben Hogan	39	9	4	2	1		2	4	2		2		1		3											
2 – Sam Snead	37	7		4	1		3	2	3	2	2	3														
3 – Byron Nelson	26	5	1	1			2	2	2	3	1	1	1	1	1											
4 – Ralph Guldahl	15	3	2	1			1	2			3															
5 – Cary Middlecoff	13	3	2	1			1	1			1	1			x											
6 – Craig Wood	13	2	1	1		1	1	2			1		1	1												
7 – Denny Shute	12	3		2	1				2	1																
8 – Jimmy Demaret	11	3		1			3				1															
9 – Henry Picard	10	2					1		1					2	2											
10 – Paul Runyon	9	2							2					1	2											

AMATEURS	TOTAL POINTS	TOTAL MAJORS WON	NATIONAL OPEN	R/U NATIONAL OPEN	BRITISH OPEN	R/U BRITISH OPEN	MASTERS	R/U MASTERS	U.S. PGA	R/U U.S. PGA	WESTERN OPEN	CANADIAN OPEN	WORLDS CHAMPION	METROPOLITAN OPEN	NORTH & SOUTH OPEN	NATIONAL AMATEUR	R/U NATIONAL AMATEUR	BRITISH AMATEUR	R/U BRITISH AMATEUR	WESTERN AMATEUR	NORTH & SOUTH AMATEUR	METROPOLITAN AMATEUR	CANADIAN AMATEUR	PACIFIC NORTHWEST AMATEUR	TRANS-MISSISSIPPI AMATEUR	FRENCH OPEN AMATEUR
1 – Frank Stranahan	22	2				2		1									1	2	1	4	3		2		1	
2 – Lawson Little	12	4	x									x				2		2								
3 – Harvie Ward	12	3														2		1	1		1		1			
4 – Willie Turnesa	11	3														2		1	1			1				
5 – Richard Chapman	11	2														1		1	2			1				2
6 – Marvin Ward	11	2														2					3			2		
7 – George Dunlap	11	1														1					7	1				
8 – Johnny Goodman	10	2	1													1	1								3	
9 – Jack Westland	10	1														1	1				1			4		1
10 – Charles Coe	9	1														1			1	1					4	

COMPUTATION OF POINTS

3 points for each Major tournament victory.
1 point for each Major tournament runner-up.
1 point for each Semi-major tournament victory.

ALL-TIME LEADERS
ALL-TIME LEADERS, 1885-1958

Column groups (left to right): **MAJORS** — National Open through R/U Professional U.S. & G.B.; **S-MAJORS** — Western Open through French Open & Amateur; **MAJORS** — National Amateur through R/U British Amateur; **S-MAJORS** — Western Amateur through Pacific Northwest-Southern & Trans-Mississippi.

PROFESSIONALS	TOTAL POINTS	TOTAL MAJORS WON	NATIONAL OPEN	R/U NATIONAL OPEN	BRITISH OPEN	R/U BRITISH OPEN	MASTERS TOURNAMENT	R/U MASTERS	PROFESSIONAL G/C – U.S. & G.B.	R/U PROFESSIONAL U.S. & G.B.	WESTERN OPEN	CANADIAN OPEN	METROPOLITAN OPEN	NORTH & SOUTH OPEN	WORLD'S CHAMPIONSHIP (72)	FRENCH OPEN & AMATEUR	NATIONAL AMATEUR	R/U NATIONAL AMATEUR	BRITISH AMATEUR	R/U BRITISH AMATEUR	WESTERN AMATEUR	CANADIAN AMATEUR	METROPOLITAN AMATEUR	NORTH & SOUTH AMATEUR	IRISH AMATEUR	PACIFIC NORTHWEST-SOUTHERN & TRANS-MISSISSIPPI
1 – Walter Hagen	49	11	2	1	4	1			5	1	5	1	3	3		1										
2 – Ben Hogan	39	9	4	2	1		2	4	2		2			3	1											
3 – Sam Snead	37	7		4	1		3	2	3	2	2	3		3												
4 – Harry Vardon	28	7	1	2	6	4					1															
5 – Gene Sarazen	27	7	2	2	1	1	1		3	1	1		1													
6 – Byron Nelson	27	5	1	1			2	2	2	3	1	1	1	1	1	1										
7 – John H. Taylor	26	5		1	5	6			2							2										
8 – James Braid	23	5			5	3			4							1										
9 – James M. Barnes	19	4	1		1	1			2	2	3			1												
10 – Willie Anderson	17	4	4	1							4															
11 – Tommy D. Armour	15	3	1		1				1	1	1	3	1													
12 – Ralph Guldahl	15	3	2	1			1	2			3															
13 – Bobby Locke	15	4		4	1							1				1										
14 – Alex Smith	15	2	2	3								2	4													
15 – T. Henry Cotton	14	3			3				3							2										
16 – Cary Middlecoff	13	3	2	1			1	1			1	1														
17 – Craig Wood	13	2	1	1			1	1	1		1		1			1										
AMATEURS																										
1 – Bobby Jones	48	13	4	4	3												5	2	1							3
2 – John Ball	34	9			1	1													8	3					3	
3 – Harold H. Hilton	28	7		2													1		4	3					4	
4 – Charles Evans	23	3	1	1												1	2	3			8		1			
5 – Jerome D. Travers	21	5	1														4	1					5			
6 – Walter J. Travis	20	4		1													3		1				4	3		
7 – Frank Stranahan	18	2				2		1										1	2	1	3	2		1		1
8 – H. Chandler Egan	15	2															2	1			4					4
9 – Francis Ouimet	13	3	1												⁹	1	2	1			1			1		
10 – Lawson Little	12	4	x												x		2		2							
11 – H. Harvie Ward	12	3															2		1	1		1		1		
12 – Willie Turnesa	11	3															2		1	1			1			
13 – Richard D. Chapman	11	2														2	1		1	2	1					
14 – Marvin Ward	11	2															2				3					(3)
15 – George T. Dunlap	11	1															1						1	7		

COMPUTATION OF POINTS

3 points for each Major tournament victory.
1 point   for each Major tournament runner-up.
1 point   for each Semi-Major tournament victory.

ALL TIME LEADERS
ALL TIME U.S. PROFESSIONAL LEADERS UP TO 1968

The listed leading U.S. Professionals are statistically based on their records of Major and Semi-major tournaments. The Semi-major events are quite ambiguous in this new era as tournaments have changed considerably.

UNITED STATES PROFESSIONALS — THE LEADERS	TOTAL POINTS	TOTAL MAJORS WON	MAJOR EVENTS								SEMI-MAJORS					
			NATIONAL OPEN WINNER	NATIONAL OPEN R/U	BRITISH OPEN WINNER	BRITISH OPEN R/U	THE MASTERS WINNER	THE MASTERS R/U	P.G.A. CHAMP., WINNER	P.G.A. CHAMP., R/U	WESTERN OPEN WINNER	CANADIAN OPEN WINNER	METROPOLITAN OPEN WINNER	NORTH & SOUTH OPEN WINNER	WORLD'S CHAMP., WINNER	FRENCH OPEN WINNER
1 – WALTER HAGEN	50	11	2	1	4	1	X	X	5	1	5	1	4	3	X	1
2 – BEN HOGAN	40	9	4	2	1	0	2	4	2	0	2	0	0	3	2	0
3 – SAM SNEAD	38	7	0	4	1	0	3	2	3	2	2	3	0	3	1	0
4 – ARNOLD PALMER	32	7	1	4	2	1	4	2	0	1	2	1	X	X	X	0
5 – JACK NICKLAUS	27	7	2	0	1	2	3	1	1	2	1	0	X	X	X	0
6 – GENE SARAZEN	29	7	2	2	1	1	1	0	3	1	1	0	3	0	X	0
7 – BYRON NELSON	27	5	1	1	0	0	2	2	2	3	1	1	1	1	1	1
8 – JAMES BARNES	19	4	1	0	1	1	X	X	2	2	3	0	0	1	X	0
9 – WILLIE ANDERSON	17	4	4	1	0	0	X	X	X	X	4	0	0	0	X	0
10 – TOMMY ARMOUR	15	3	1	0	1	0	X	X	1	1	1	3	1	1	X	0
11 – RALPH GULDAHL	15	3	2	1	0	0	1	2	0	0	3	0	0	0	X	0
12 – CARY MIDDLECOFF	14	3	2	1	0	0	1	1	0	1	1	0	X	1	X	0
13 – DENNY SHUTE	13	3	0	2	1	0	0	0	2	1	0	0	0	0	X	0
14 – JIMMY DEMARET	11	3	0	1	0	0	3	0	0	0	1	0	0	X	0	0

COMPUTATION OF POINTS

Three points for each Major tournament victory.
One point for each Major tournament runner-up.
One point for each Semi-major tournament victory.

X indicates the events in which the Pro did not participate. In most cases, these events were non-existent during the Pro's career.

The Metropolitan, North and South and the World's (Tam O'Shanter) events, have been discontinued, and in the modern era other events would no doubt be considered as Semi-majors, sich as: the Colonial National, Tournament of Champions, etc.

THE IMMORTAL GOLFERS OF THE WORLD
ALL TIME IMMORTALS UP TO 1968

PROFESSIONALS	The year in which the fourth major title was attained	Total number of major titles won	Percentage of tournaments won in which the competitor was eligible to participate	Span of years in which titles were won (From 1st to 4th)	REMARKS
(Old) Tom Morris	1867	4	100	7	Gutta Percha Period
(Young) Tommy Morris, Jr.	1872	4	100	5	Gutta Percha Period
William (Willie) Park	1875	4	100	16	Gutta Percha Period
Harry Vardon	1900	7	100	5	"Gutties" and Rubber Ball Era
Willie Anderson	1905	4	50	5	"Gutties" and Rubber Ball Era
James Braid	1908	5	50	8	"Gutties" and Rubber Ball Era
John H. Taylor	1909	5	50	16	"Gutties" and Rubber Ball Era
Walter Hagen	1924	11	100	8	Rubber Ball and Hickory Shaft Era
James Barnes	1925	4	100	10	Rubber Ball and Hickory Shaft Era
Gene Sarazen	1932	7	100	11	Hickory and Steel Shaft Era
Byron Nelson	1942	5	75	6	Steel Shaft Era
Sam Snead	1949	7	75	8	Steel Shaft Era
Ben Hogan	1950	9	100	5	Steel Shaft Era
Bobby Locke	1957	4	50	9	Steel Shaft Era
Peter Thomsom	1958	5	50	5	Steel Shaft Era
Arnold Palmer	1961	7	75	5	Steel Shaft Era
Jack Nicklaus	1965	7	100	4	Steel Shaft Era
Gary Player	1965	4	100	7	Steel Shaft Era
AMATEURS					
John Ball	1892	9	50	5	"Gutties" and Rubber Ball Era
Harold H. Hilton	1901	7	75	10	"Gutties" and Rubber Ball Era
Walter J. Travis	1903	4	50	5	"Gutties" and Rubber Ball Era
Jerome D. Travers	1913	5	50	7	Rubber Ball and Hickory Shaft Era
Robert T. Jones, Jr.	1926	13	100	4	Hickory and Steel Shaft Era
W. Lawson Little, Jr.	1935	4	50	2	Steel Shaft Era

The author bases the validity of his ratings on a golfer's achievement of winning four major championships. Placed in the order of the year in which the competitor won his fourth major title, the mark of "immortality."

Year	Winner	Score	Runner-up	Held At
1895	Horace Rawlins	173-36 holes	Willie Dunn	Newport Golf Club
1896	James Foulis	152-36 holes	Horace Rawlins	Shinnecock Hills G. C.
1897	Joe Lloyd	162-36 holes	Willie Anderson	Chicago Golf Club
1898	Fred Herd	328-72 holes	Alex Smith	Myopia Club
1899	Willie Smith	315	George Low, Val Fitzjohn, W. H. Way	Baltimore Country Club
1900	Harry Vardon	313	J. H. Taylor	Chicago Golf Club
1901	*Willie Anderson (85)	331	Alex Smith (86)	Myopia Hunt Club
1902	Lawrence Auchterlonie	307	Stewart Gardner and W. J. Travis	Garden City Golf Club
1903	*Willie Anderson (82)	307	David Brown (84)	Baltusrol Golf Club
1904	Willie Anderson	303	Gil Nicholls	Glen View Club
1905	Willie Anderson	314	Alex Smith	Myopia Hunt Club
1906	Alex Smith	295	Willie Smith	Onwentsia Club
1907	Alex Ross	302	Gil Nicholls	Philadelphia Cricket Club
1908	*Fred McLeod (77)	322	Willie Smith (83)	Myopia Hunt Club
1909	George Sargent	290	Tom McNamara	Englewood Golf Club
1910	*Alex Smith (71)	298	J.J. McDermott (75) and Macdonald Smith (77)	Philadelphia Cricket Club
1911	*John J. McDermott (80)	307	Michael J. Brady (82) and George O. Simpson (85)	Chicago Golf Club
1912	John J. McDermott	294	Tom McNamara	Country Club of Buffalo
1913	*Francis Ouimet (76)	304	Vardon (77), Ray (78)	The Country Club, Brookline
1914	Walter Hagen	290	Charles Evans, Jr.	Midlothian Country Club
1915	Jerome D. Travers	297	Tom McNamara	Baltusrol Golf Club
1916	Charles Evans, Jr.	286	Jock Hutchison	Minikahda Club
1917 & 1918—No Championships played—World War I.				
1919	*Walter Hagen (77)	301	Michael J. Brady (78)	Brae Burn Country Club
1920	Edward Ray	295	Harry Vardon, Jack Burke,	Inverness Club
1921	James M. Barnes	289	Leo Diegel, Jock Hutchison Walter Hagen, Fred McLeod	Columbia Country Club
1922	Gene Sarazen	288	Robert T. Jones, Jr., John L. Black	Skokie Country Club
1923	*Robert T. Jones, Jr. (76)	296	Robert A. Cruickshank (78)	Inwood Country Club
1924	Cyril Walker	297	Robert T. Jones, Jr.	Oakland Hills Country Club
1925	*Willie Macfarlane (75-72)	291	Robert T. Jones, Jr. (75-73)	Worcester Country Club
1926	Robert T. Jones, Jr.	293	Joe Turnesa	Scioto Country Club
1927	*Tommy Armour (76)	301	Harry Cooper (79)	Oakmont Country Club
1928	*Johnny Farrell (143)	294	Robert T. Jones, Jr. (144)	Olympia Fields C. C.
1929	*Robert T. Jones, Jr. (141)	294	Al Espinosa (164)	Winged Foot Golf Club
1930	Robert T. Jones, Jr.	287	Macdonald Smith	Interlachen Country Club
1931	*Billy Burke (149-148)	292	George Von Elm (149-149)	Inverness Club
1932	Gene Sarazen	286	Robert A. Cruickshank	Fresh Meadow C. C.
1933	John G. Goodman	287	T. Philip Perkins	
1934	Olin Dutra	293	Ralph Guldahl	North Shore Golf Club
1935	Sam Parks, Jr.	299	Gene Sarazen Jommy Thomson	Merion Cricket Club Oakmont Country Club
1936	Tony Manero	282	Harry E. Cooper	Baltusrol Golf Club
1937	Ralph Guldahl	281	Sam Snead	Oakland Hills Country Club
1938	Ralph Guldahl	284	Dick Metz	Cherry Chills Club
1939	*Byron Nelson (68-70)	284	Craig Wood (68-73) Denny Shute (76-elim.)	Philadelphia Country Club
1940	*Lawson Little (70)	287	Gene Sarazen (73)	Canterbury Golf Club
1941	Craig Wood	284	Denny Shute	Colonial Club
1942-43-44-45—No Championships played—World War II.				
1946	*Lloyd Mangrum (72-72)	284	Ghezzi(72-73), Nelson(72-73)	Canterbury G. C.
1947	*Lew Worsham (69)	282	Sam Snead (70)	St. Louis C. C.

211

1948	Ben Hogan	276	Jimmy Demaret	Riviera C. C.
1949	Cary Middlecoff	286	Sam Snead, Clayton Heafner	Medinah C. C.
1950	*Ben Hogan (69)	287	Mangrum (73), Fazio (75)	Merion C. C.
1951	Ben Hogan	287	Clayton Heafner	Oakland Hills C. C.
1952	Julius Boros	281	Ed (Porky) Oliver	Northwood C. C.
1953	Ben Hogan	283	Sam Snead	Oakmont C. C.
1954	Ed Furgol	284	Gene Littler	Baltusrol G. C.
1955	*Jack Fleck (69)	287	Ben Hogan (72)	Olympic C. C.
1956	Cary Middlecoff	281	Julius Boros, Ben Hogan	Oak Hills C. C.
1957	*Dick Mayer (72)	282	Cary Middlecoff (79)	Inverness Club
1958	Tommy Bolt	283	Gary Player	Southern Hills C. C.
1959	Billy Casper, Jr.	282	Bob Rosburg	Winged Foot G. C.
1960	Arnold Palmer	280	Jack Nicklaus	Cherry Hills C. C.
1961	Gene Littler	281	Doug Sanders	Oakland Hills C. C.
1962	*Jack Nicklaus (71)	283	Arnold Palmer (74)	Oakmont (Pa.) C. C.
1963	*Julius Boros (70)	293	Arnold Palmer (76) Jack Cupit (73)	The Country Club
1964	Ken Venturi	278	Tommy Jacobs	Congressional C. C.
1965	*Gary Player (71)	282	Kel Nagle (74)	Bellerive C. C.
*1966	Billy Casper (69)	278	Arnold Palmer (73) 278	Olympic Club
1967	Jack Nicklaus	275	Arnold Palmer 279	Baltusrol G. C.

*Winner on play-off. Figures in parentheses are scores in play-off.

(From the Records of The United States Golf Association)

THE BRITISH OPEN CHAMPIONSHIP

Year	Winner	Score	Held At
1860	W. Park, Musselburgh	163	Prestwick
1861	Tom Morris, Sr., Prestwick	163	Prestwick
1862	Tom Morris, Sr., Prestwick	174	Prestwick
1863	W. Park, Musselburgh	168	Prestwick
1864	Tom Morris, Sr.,	167	Prestwick
1865	A. Strath, St. Andrews	162	Prestwick
1866	W. Park, Musselburgh	169	Prestwick
1867	Tom Morris, Sr., St. Andrews	170	Prestwick
1868	Tom Morris, Jr., St. Andrews	170	Prestwick
1869	Tom Morris, Jr., St. Andrews	157	Prestwick
1870	Tom Morris, Jr., St. Andrews	149	Prestwick
1871	No Championship		
1872	Tom Morris, Jr., St. Andrews	166	Prestwick
1873	Tom Kidd, St. Andrews	179	St. Andrews
1874	Mungo Park, Musselburgh	159	Musselburgh
1875	Willie Park, Musselburgh	166	Prestwick
1876	Bob Martin, St. Andrews	176	St. Andrews
1877	Jamie Anderson, St. Andrews	160	Musselburgh
1878	Jamie Anderson, St. Andrews	157	Prestwick
1879	Jamie Anderson, St. Andrews	170	St. Andrews
1880	Bob Ferguson, Musselburgh	162	Musselburgh
1881	Bob Ferguson, Musselburgh	170	Prestwick
1882	Bob Ferguson, Musselburgh	171	St. Andrews
1883	*Wm. Fernie, Dumfries	159	Musselburgh
1884	Jack Simpson, Carnoustic	160	Prestwick
1885	Bob Martin, St. Andrews	171	St. Andrews
1886	D. Brown, Musselburgh	157	Musselburgh
1887	W. Park, Jr., Musselburgh	161	Prestwick
1888	Jack Burns, Warwick	171	St. Andrews

1889	*W. Park, Jr., Musselburgh	155	Musselburgh
1890	**John Ball, Royal Liverpool	164	Prestwick
1891	Hugh Kirkaldy, St. Andrews	166	St. Andrews
1892	**H. H. Hilton, Royal Liverpool	305	Muirfield
1893	W. Auchterlonie, St. Andrews	322	Prestwick
1894	J. H. Taylor, Winchester	326	Sandwich
1895	J. H. Taylor, Winchester	322	St. Andrews
1896	*Harry Vardon, Ganton	316	Muirfield
1897	**H. H. Hilton, Royal Liverpool	314	Hoylake
1898	Harry Vardon, Ganton	307	Sandwich
1899	Harry Vardon, Ganton	310	Sandwich
1900	J. H. Taylor, Mid-Surrey	309	St. Andrews
1901	James Braid, Romford	309	Muirfield
1902	Alex Herd, Huddersfield	307	Hoylake
1903	Harry Vardon, Totteridge	300	Prestwick
1904	Jack White, Sunningdale	296	Sandwich
1905	James Braid, Walton Heath	300	Muirfield
1906	James Braid, Walton Heath	300	Muirfield
1907	Arnaud Massy, La Boulie	312	Hoylake
1908	James Braid, Walton Heath	291	Prestwick
1909	J. H. Taylor, Mid-Surrey	295	Deal
1910	James Braid, Walton Heath	299	St. Andrews
1911	Harry Vardon, Totteridge	303	Sandwich
1912	E. Ray, Oxhey	295	Muirfield
1913	J. H. Taylor, Mid-Surrey	304	Hoylake
1914	Harry Vardon, Totteridge	306	Prestwick
1915-19	No Championships because of World War I		
1920	George Duncan, Hanger Hill	303	Deal
1921	Jock Hutchison, U.S.A.	296	St. Andrews
1922	Walter Hagen, U.S.A.	300	Sandwich
1923	A. G. Havers, Coombe Hill	295	Troon
1924	Walter Hagen, U.S.A.	301	Hoylake
1925	Jim Barnes, U.S.A.	300	Prestwick
1926	Robert Jones, Jr., U.S.A.	291	Royal Lytham and St. Anne's
1927	**Robert Jones, Jr., U.S.A.	285	St. Andrews
1928	Walter Hagen, U.S.A.	292	Sandwich
1929	Walter Hagen, U.S.A.	292	Muirfield and Gullane
1930	Robert Jones, Jr., U.S.A.	291	Hoylake
1931	Tommy Armour, U.S.A.	296	Carnoustie
1932	Gene Sarazen, U.S.A.	283	Sandwich
1933	*Denny Shute, U.S.A.	292	St. Andrews
1934	Henry Cotton, Waterloo	283	Sandwich
1935	Alf Perry, Leatherhead	283	Muirfield
1936	Alfred Padgham, Sundridge Park	287	Hoylake
1937	Henry Cotton, Ashridge	290	Carnoustie
1938	Reginald A. Whitcombe	295	Sandwich
1939	Richard Burton, Sale	290	St. Andrews
1940-45	No Championships		
1946	Sam Snead, U.S.A.	290	St. Andrews
1947	Fred Daly	293	Hoylake
1948	Henry Cotton	284	Muirfield
1949	*Bobby Locke	283	St. George
1950	Bobby Locke	279	Troon
1951	Max Faulkner	285	Portrush
1952	Bobby Locke	287	Royal Lytham and St. Anne's
1953	Ben Hogan	282	Carnoustie
1954	Peter Thomson	283	Birkdale
1955	Peter Thomson	281	St. Andrews

1956	Peter Thomson	286	Hoylake
1957	Bobby Locke	279	St. Andrews
1958	*Peter Thomson	278	St. Anne's
1959	Gary Player	284	Muirfield
1960	Ken Nagle	278	St. Andrews
1961	Arnold Palmer	284	Birkdale
1962	Arnold Palmer	276	Troon
1963	*Bob Charles	277	St. Anne's
1964	Tony Lema	279	St. Andrews
1965	Peter Thomson	285	Birkdale
1966	Jack Nicklaus	282	Muirfield
1967	Roberto De Vicenzo	278	Hoylake

*Winner in play-off.
**Denotes amateur.

NATIONAL PROFESSIONAL GOLFERS CHAMPIONSHIP

Year	Winner	Score	Runnerup	Played At
1916	James M. Barnes	1 up	Jock Hutchison	Siwanoy Country Club, Bronxville, N.Y.
1917-1918 NO CHAMPIONSHIP PLAYED—WORLD WAR I				
1919	James M. Barnes	6 & 5	Fred McLeod	Engineers Country Club, Roslyn, L.I., N.Y.
1920	Jock Hutchison	1 up	J. Douglas Edgar	Flossmoor Country Club, Flossmoor, Ill.
1921	Wlter Hagen	3 & 2	James M. Barnes	Inwood Country Club, Far Rockaway, N.Y.
1922	Gene Sarazen	4 & 3	Emmet French	Oakmont Country Club, Oakmont, Pa.
1923	Gene Sarazen	1 up (38)	Walter Hagen	Pelham Country Club, Pelham, N.Y.
1924	Walter Hagen	2 up	James M. Barnes	French Lick Country Club, French Lick, Ind.
1925	Walter Hagen	6 & 5	William Mehlhorn	Olympia Fields Country Club, Olympia Fields, Ill.
1926	Walter Hagen	5 & 3	Leo Diegel	Salisbury Golf Club, Westbury, L.I., N.Y.
1927	Walter Hagen	1 up	Joe Turnesa	Cedar Crest Country Club, Dallas, Texas
1928	Leo Diegel	6 & 5	Al Espinosa	Five Farms Country Club, Baltimore, Md.
1929	Leo Diegel	6 & 4	Johnny Farrell	Hillcrest Country Club, Los Angeles, Calif.
1930	Tommy Armour	1 up	Gene Sarazen	Fresh Meadows Country Club, Flushing, N.Y.
1931	Tom Creavy	2 & 1	Denny Shute	Wannamoisett Country Club, Rumford, R.I.
1932	Olin Dutra	4 & 3	Frank Walsh	Keller Golf Club, St. Paul, Minn.
1933	Gene Sarazen	5 & 4	Willie Goggin	Blue Mound Country Club, Milwaukee, Wis.
1934	Paul Runyan	1 up (38)	Craig Wood	Park Country Club, Williamsville, N.Y.
1935	Johnny Revolta	5 & 4	Tommy Armour	Twin Hills Country Club, Oklahoma City, Okla.
1936	Denny Shute	3 & 2	Jimmy Thomson	Pinehurst Country Club, Pinehurst, N.C.
1937	Denny Shute	1 up (37)	Harold McSpaden	Pittsburgh Field Club, Aspinwall, Pa.
1938	Paul Runyan	8 & 7	Sam Snead	Shawnee Country Club, Shawnee-on-Delaware, Pa.
1939	Henry Picard	1 up (37)	Byron Nelson	Pomonok Country Club, Flushing, L.I., N.Y.
1940	Byron Nelson	1 up	Sam Snead	Hershey Country Club, Hershey, Pa.
1941	Vic Ghezzi	1 up (38)	Byron Nelson	Cherry Hills Country Club, Denver, Colo.
1942	Sam Snead	2 & 1	Jim Turnesa	Seaview Country Club, Atlantic City, N.J.
1943 NO CHAMPIONSHIP PLAYED—WORLD WAR II				
1944	Bob Hamilton	1 up	Byron Nelson	Manito Golf & Country Club, Spokane, Wash.
1945	Byron Nelson	4 & 3	Sam Byrd	Morraine Country Club, Dayton, Ohio
1946	Ben Hogan	6 & 4	Ed Oliver	Portland Golf Club, Portland, Ore.
1947	Jim Ferrier	2 & 1	Chick Harbert	Plum Hollow Country Club, Detroit, Mich.
1948	Ben Hogan	7 & 6	Mike Turnesa	Norwood Hills Country Club, St. Louis, Mo.
1949	Sam Snead	3 & 2	Johnny Palmer	Hermitage Country Club, Richmond, Va.
1950	Chandler Harper	4 & 3	Henry Williams, Jr.	Scioto Country Club, Columbus, Ohio
1951	Sam Snead	7 & 6	Walter Burkemo	Oakmont Country Club, Oakmont, Pa.

1952	Jim Turnesa	1 up	Chick Harbert	Big Spring Country Club, Louisville, Ky.
1953	Walter Burkemo	2 & 1	Felice Torza	Birmingham Country Club, Birmingham, Mich.
1954	Chick Harbert	4 & 3	Walter Burkemo	Keller Golf Club, St. Paul, Minn.
1955	Doug Ford	4 & 3	Cary Middlecoff	Meadowbrook Country Club, Detroit, Mich.
1956	Jack Burke, Jr.	3 & 2	Ted Kroll	Blue Hill Country Club, Boston, Mass.
1957	Lionel Hebert	2 & 1	Dow Finsterwald	Miami Valley Golf Club, Dayton, Ohio
1958	Dow Finsterwald	276	Bill Casper, Jr.	Llanerch Country Club, Havertown, Pa.
1959	Bob Rosburg	277	Jerry Barber Doug Sanders	Minneapolis Golf Club, St. Louis Park, Minn.
1960	Jay Hebert	281	Jim Ferrier	Firestone Country Club, Akron, Ohio
1961	*Jerry Barber	277 (67)	Don January (68)	Olympia Fields Country Club, Olympia Fields, Ill.
1962	Gary Player	278	Bob Goalby	Aronimink Golf Club, Newtown Square, Pa.
1963	Jack Nicklaus	279	Dave Ragan, Jr.	Dallas Athletic Club Country Club, Dallas, Texas
1964	Bob Nichols	271	Arnold Palmer Jack Nicklaus	Columbus Country Club, Columbus, Ohio
1965	Dave Marr	280	Bill Casper, Jr. Jack Nicklaus	Laurel Valley Golf Club, Ligonier, Pa.
1966	Al Geiberger	280	Dudley Wysong	Firestone Country Club, Akron, Ohio
1967	*Don January	281 (69)	Don Massengale (71)	Columbine Country Club, Denver, Colorado

*Winner in playoff

(From the Records of the Professional Golfers Association)

MASTERS TOURNAMENT
Augusta National Golf Club, Augusta, Georgia

Year	Winner	Score	Runner-Up	Score
1934	Horton Smith	284	Craig Wood	285
1935	*Gene Sarazen (144)	282	Craig Wood (149)	282
1936	Horton Smith	285	Harry Cooper	286
1937	Byron Nelson	283	Ralph Guldahl	285
1938	Henry Picard	285	Ralph Guldahl	287
1939	Ralph Guldahl	279	Sam Snead	280
1940	Jimmy Demaret	280	Lloyd Mangrum	284
1941	Craig Wood	280	Byron Nelson	283
1942	*Byron Nelson (69)	280	Ben Hogan (70)	280
1943-45	No Tournaments played			
1946	Herman Keiser	282	Ben Hogan	283
1947	Jimmy Demaret	281	Byron Nelson	283
1948	Claude Harmon	279	Cary Middlecoff	284
1949	Sam Snead	282	Lloyd Mangrum Johnny Bulla	285
1950	Jimmy Demaret	283	Jim Ferrier	285
1951	Ben Hogan	280	Skee Riegel	282
1952	Sam Snead	286	Jack Burke, Jr.	290
1953	Ben Hogan	274	Ed (Porky) Oliver	279
1954	*Sam Snead (70)	289	Ben Hogan (71)	289
1955	Cary Middlecoff	279	Ben Hogan	286
1956	Jack Burke, Jr.	289	**Ken Venturi	290

1957	Doug Ford	283	Sam Snead	286
1958	Arnold Palmer	284	Doug Ford	285
1959	Art Wall	284	Fred Hawkins	285
1960	Arnold Palmer	282	Ken Venturi	283
1961	G. Player	280	A. Palmer	281
			**C. Coe	
1962	*Arnold Palmer (68)	280	G. Player (71)	280
			D. Finsterwald (77)	
1963	Jack Nicklaus	286	T. Lema	287
1964	Arnold Palmer	276	Jack Nicklaus	282
			Dave Marr	
1965	Jack Nicklaus	271	Arnold Palmer,	280
			Gary Player	
1966	*Jack Nicklaus (70)	288	Tommy Jacobs (72)	
			Gay Brewer (78)	
1967	Gay Brewer	280	Bobby Nichols	281

*Play-Off   **Amateur

(From the Records of the Augusta National Golf Club)

THE UNITED STATES WOMEN'S OPEN CHAMPIONSHIP

Year	Winner	Score	Runner-up	Held At
1946	*Miss Patty Berg	5 & 4	Miss Betty Jameson	Spokane, Wash.
1947	Miss Betty Jameson	295	Miss Sally Sessions	Greensboro, N.C.
			Miss Polly Riley	
1948	Mrs. George Zaharias	300	Miss Betty Hicks	Atlantic City, N. J.
1949	Miss Louise Suggs	291	Mrs. George Zaharias	Landover, Md.
1950	Mrs. George Zaharias	291	Miss Betsy Rawls	Wichita, Kansas
1951	Miss Betsy Rawls	293	Miss Louise Suggs	Atlanta, Ga.
1952	Miss Louise Suggs	284	Miss Betty Jameson	Bala, Pa.
			Miss Marlene Bauer	
1953	**Miss Betsy Rawls (71)	302	Mrs. Jacqueline Pung (77)	Rochester (N.Y.) C. C.
1954	Mrs. George Zaharias	291	Miss Betty Hicks	Salem (Mass.) C. C.
1955	Miss Fay Crocker	299	Miss Louise Suggs	Wichita (Kans.) C. C.
1956	**Mrs. Kathy Cornelius (75)	302	Miss Barbara McIntire (82)	Northland C. C., Duluth, Minn.
1957	Miss Betsy Rawls	299	Miss Patty Berg	Winged Foot G. C., Mamaroneck, N.Y.

*Match Play.   **Winner in play-off.

1958	Miss Mickey Wright	290	Miss Louise Suggs	Forest Lake C. C., Detroit, Mich.
1959	Miss Mickey Wright	287	Miss Louise Suggs	Churchill Valley C. C., Pittsburgh, Pa.
1960	Miss Betsy Rawls	292	Miss Joyce Ziske	Worcester (Mass.) C. C.
1961	Miss Mickey Wright	293	Miss Betsy Rawls	Baltusrol G. C., Springfield, N. J.
1962	Miss Murle Lindstrom	301	Miss Jo Ann Prentice	Dunes G. C.
			Miss Ruth Jessen	Myrtle Beach, S. C.
1963	Miss Mary Mills	289	Miss Sandra Haynie	Kenwood C. C., Cincinnati, Ohio
			Miss Louise Suggs	
1964	Miss Mickey Wright	290	Miss Ruth Jessen	San Diego C. C.
	(Winner in Play-off 70-72)			

1965	Carol Mann	290	Kathy Cornelius (292)	Atlantic City C. C.
1966	Sandra Spuzich	297	Carol Mann (298)	Hazeltine Nat'l. C. C., Chaska, Minn.
1967 X	Catherine Lacoste	294	Suzie Maxwell (296)	Homestead G. C.
			Beth Stone (296)	Hot Springs, Va.

X Amateur

(From the Records of the United States Golf Association)

LADIES' PROFESSIONAL GOLFERS CHAMPIONSHIP

Year	Winner	Score	Runner-up	Score	Held at
1955	Beverly Hanson	4 & 3	Louise Suggs		Orchard Ridge C.C. Fort Wayne, Ind.
1956	*Marlene Hagge	291	Patty Berg	291	Forest Lake C. C. Detroit, Mich.
1957	Louise Suggs	285	Wiffi Smith	288	Churchill Valley C. C. Pittsburgh, Pa.
1958	Mickey Wright	288	Fay Crocker	294	Churchill Valley C. C. Pittsburgh, Pa.
1959	Betsy Rawls	288	Patty Berg	289	Sheraton Hotel C. C. French Lick, Ind.
1960	Mickey Wright	292	Louise Suggs	295	Sheraton Hotel C.C. French Lick, Ind.
1961	Mickey Wright	287	Louise Suggs	296	Stardust C.C. Las Vegas, Nev.
1962	Judy Kimball	282	Shirley Spork	286	Stardust C.C. Las Vegas, Nev.
1963	Mickey Wright	294	Mary Lena Faulk Mary Mills Louise Suggs	296	Stardust C.C. Las Vegas, Nev.
1964	Mary Mills	278	Mickey Wright	280	Stardust C.C. Las Vegas, Nev.
1965	Sandra Haynie	279	Clifford Ann Creed	280	Stardust C.C. Las Vegas, Nev.
1966	Gloria Ehret	282	Mickey Wright	285	Stardust C.C. Las Vegas, Nev.
1967	Kathy Whitworth	284	Shirley Englehorn	285	Pleasent Valley C.C. Sutton, Mass.

*Winner in playoff.

(From the records of the Ladies Professional Golfers Association)

UNITED STATES NATIONAL AMATEUR CHAMPIONSHIP

USGA MEN'S NATIONAL AMATEUR

Year	Site	Winner, Runner-up	Score
1895	Newport G.C. Newport, R.I.	Charles B. Macdonald d. C. E. Sands	12 and 11
1896	Shinnecock Southampton, N.Y.	H.J. Whigham d. J. G. Throp	8 and 7
1897	Chicago G.C. Wheaton, Ill.	H.J. Whigham d. W. R. Betts	8 and 6
1898	Morris County G.C. Morristown, N.J.	Findley S. Douglas d. W. B. Smith	5 and 3
1899	Onwentsia Club Lake Forest, Ill.	H. M. Harriman d. F. S. Douglas	3 and 2
1900	Garden City (N.Y.) G.C.	Walter J. Travis d. F. S. Douglas	2 up
1901	C.C. of Atlantic City, N.J.	Walter J. Travis d. W. E. Egan	5 and 4
1902	Glen View Golf, Ill.	Louis N. James d. E. M. Byers	4 and 2
1903	Nassau C.C. Glen Cove, N.Y.	Walter J. Travis d. E. M. Byers	5 and 4
1904	Baltusrol G.C. Springfield, N.J.	H. Chandler Egan d. F. Herreshoff	8 and 6
1905	Chicago G.C. Wheaton, Ill.	H. Chandler Egan d. D. E. Sawyer	6 and 5
1906	Englewood (N.J.) G.C.	Eben M. Byers d. G. S. Lyon	2 up
1907	Euclid Club Cleveland, O.	Jerome D. Travers d. A. Graham	6 and 5
1908	Garden City (N.Y.) G.C.	Jerome D. Travers d. Max H. Behr	8 and 7
1909	Chicago G.C. Wheaton, Ill.	Robert A. Gardner d. H. C. Egan	4 and 3
1910	The Country Club Brookline, Mass.	William C. Fownes, Jr. d. W. K. Wood	4 and 3
1911	The Apawamis C., Rye, N.Y.	Harold H. Hilton d. F. Her'shoff	1 up, 37 hls.
1912	Chicago G.C. Wheaton, Ill.	Jerome D. Travers d. C. Evans, Jr.	7 and 6
1913	Garden City (N.Y.) G.C.	Jerome D. Travers d. J. G. Anderson	5 and 4
1914	Ekwanok C.C. Manchester, Vt.	Francis Ouimet d. J. D. Travers	6 and 5
1915	C.C. of Detroit Grosse Pointe Farms, Mich.	Robert A. Gardner d. J. G. Anderson	5 and 4
1916	Merion Cricket C. Haverford, Pa.	Charles Evans, Jr. d. R. A. Gardner	4 and 3
1917-1918 No Championships			
1919	Oakmont (Pa.) C.C.	Davidson Herron d. R. T. Jones, Jr.	5 and 4
1920	Engineers' C.C. Roslyn, N.Y.	Charles Evans, Jr. d. F. Ouimet	7 and 6
1921	St. Louis C.C. Clayton, Mo.	Jesse P. Guilford d. R. A. Gardner	7 and 6
1922	The Country Club Brookline, Mass.	Jess W. Sweetser d. C. Evans, Jr.	3 and 2

1923	Flossmoor (Ill.) C.C.	Mas R. Marston d. J. W. Sweestser	1 up, 38 hls.
1924	Merion Cricket C. Haverford, Pa.	Robert T. Jones, Jr. d. G. Von Elm	9 and 8
1925	Oakmont (Pa.) C.C.	Robert T. Jones, Jr. d. Watts Gunn	8 and 7
1926	Baltusrol G.C. Springfield, N.J.	George Von Elm d. R. T. Jones, Jr.	2 and 1
1927	Minikahda C.C. Minneapolis, Minn.	Robert T. Jones, Jr. d. C. Evans, Jr.	8 and 7
1928	Brae Burn C.C. West Newton, Mass.	Robert T. Jones, Jr. d. T. P. Perkins	10 and 9
1929	Del Monte G. & C.C., Pebble Beach Course, Cal.	d. Dr. O. F. Willing	4 and 3
1930	Merion Cricket C. Ardmore, Pa.	Robert T. Jones, Jr. d. E. V. Homans	8 and 7
1931	Beverly C.C. Chicago, Ill.	Francis Ouimet d. J. Westland	6 and 5
1932	Baltimore (Md.) C.C.	C. Ross Somerville d. J. Goodman	2 and 1
1933	Kenwood C.C. Cincinnati, O.	George T. Dunlap, Jr. d. M. Marston	6 and 5
1934	The Country Club Brookline, Mass.	W. Lawson Little, Jr. d. D. Goldman	8 and 7
1935	The Country Club Cleveland, O.	W. Lawson Little, Jr. d. W. Emery	4 and 2
1936	Garden City (N.Y.) G.C.	John W. Fischer d. J. McLean	1 up, 37 hls.
1937	Alderwood C.C. Portland, Ore.	John G. Goodman d. R. E. Billows	2 up
1938	Oakmont (Pa.) C.C.	William P. Turnesa d. B. P. Abbott	8 and 7
1939	North Shore C.C. Glenview, Ill.	Marvin H. Ward d. R. E. Billows	7 and 5
1940	Winged Foot G.C. Mamaroneck, N.Y.	Richard D. Chapman d. W. B. McCullough, Jr.	11 and 9
1941	Omaha Field C. Omaha, Neb.	Marvin H. Ward d. B. P. Abbott	4 and 3
1942-45	No championships		
1946	Baltusrol G.C. Springfield, N.J.	Stanley E. Bishop d. S. L. Quick	1 up, 37 hls.
1947	Del Monte G. & C.C., Pebble Beach Course, Cal.	Robert H. Riegel d. J. W. Dawson	2 and 1
1948	Memphis C.C. Memphis, Tenn.	William P. Turnesa d. R. E. Billows	2 and 1
1949	Oak Hill C.C. Rochester, N.Y.	Charles R. Coe d. R. King	11 and 10
1950	Minneapolis G.C. Minneapolis, Minn.	Sam Urzetta d. F. Stranahan	1 up, 39 hls.
1951	Saucon Valley C.C. Bethlehem, Pa.	Billy Maxwell d. J. F. Gagliardi	4 and 3
1952	Seattle G.C. Seattle, Wash.	Jack Westland d. Al Mengert	3 and 2
1953	Oklahoma City G. & C.C. Oklahoma City, Okla.	Gene A. Littler d. Dale Morey	1 up
1954	C.C. of Detroit Grosse Pointe Farms, Mich.	Arnold D. Palmer d. R. Sweeny	

1955	C.C. of Virginia Richmond, Va.	E. Harvie Ward d. W. Hyndman, Ill.	9 and 8
1956	Knollwood C.C. Lake Forest, Ill.	E. Harvie Ward d. C. Kocsis	5 and 4
1957	The Country Club Brookline, Mass.	Hillman Robbins d. Dr. Taylor	5 and 4
1958	Olympia C.C. San Francisco	Charles Coe d. T. Aaron	5 and 4
1959	Broadmoor G.C., Colorado Springs, Colo.	Jack Nicklaus d. Charles Coe	1 up
1960	St. Louis C.C. Clayton, Mo.	Deane Beman d. B. Gardner	6 and 4
1961	Pebble Beach (Calif.) C.C.	Jack Nicklaus d. D. Wysong, Jr.	8 and 6
1962	Pinehurst (N.C.) C.C.	Labron Harris, Jr. d. Downing Fray	1 up
1963	Wakonda C.C. Des Moines, Ia.	Deane Beman df. R. H. Sikes	2 and 1
1964	Canterbury G.C. Cleveland, O.	Bill Campbell df. Ed Tutwiler	1 up
1965	Southern Hills C.C., Tulsa, Okla	Bob Murphy Bob Dickson	291 292
1966	Merion G.C., Ardmore, Penn.	Gary Cowan Deane Beman	285-75 285-76
1967	Broadmoor C.C. Colorado Spgs., Colo.	Bob Dickson Vinnie Giles	285 286

(From the records of the United States Golf Association)

USGA WOMEN'S AMATEUR CHAMPIONSHIP

Year	Site	Winner, runner-up	Score
1895	Meadow Brook C., Hempstead, N.Y.	C. S. Brown N.C. Sargent	132 134
1896	Morris County G.C., Morristown, N.J.	Beatrix Hoyt d. Mrs. Turnure	2 and 1
1897	Essex C.C., Manchester, Mass.	Beatrix Hoyt d. N. C. Sargent	5 and 4
1898	Ardsley C., Ardsley-on-Hudson, N.Y.	Beatrix Hoyt d. M. Wetmore	5 and 3
1899	Philadelphia (Pa.) C.C.	Ruth Underhill d. C. Box	2 and 1
1900	Shinnecock Hills (N.Y.) G.C.	Frances Griscom d. M. Curtis	6 and 5
1901	Baltusrol G.C., Springfield, N.J.	Genevieve Hecker d. Lucy Herron	5 and 3
1902	The Country Club, Brookline, Mass.	Genevieve Hecker d. Louisa Wells	4 and 3
1903	Chicago, G.C., Wheaton, Ill.	Bessie Anthony d. J. A. Carpenter	7 and 6
1904	Merion Cricket C., Haverford, Pa.	Georgianna Bishop d. E. F. Sanford	5 and 3
1905	Morris County G.C., Morristown N.J.	Pauline Mackey d. M. Curtis	1 up

1906	Brae Burn C.C., Newton, Mass.	Harriot Curtis d. M. B. Adams	2 and 1
1907	Midlothian C.C., Blue Island, Ill.	Margaret Curtis d. H. Curtis	2 and 1
1908	Chevy Chase (Md.) C.	Katherine Harley d. T. H. Polhemus	6 and 5
1909	Merion Cricket C., Haverford, Pa.	Dorothy Campbell d. R. H. Barlow	3 and 2
1910	Homewood C.C., Flossmoor, Ill.	Dorothy Campbell d. G. M. Martin	2 and 1
1911	Baltusrol G.C., Springfield, N.J.	Margaret Curtis d. L. Hyde	5 and 3
1912	Essex C.C., Manchester, Mass.	Margaret Curtis d. R. H. Barlow	3 and 2
1913	Wilmington (Del.) C.C.	Gladys Ravenscroft d. M. Hollins	2 up
1914	Nassau C.C., Glen Cove, N.Y.	H.A. Jackson d. E. Rosenthal	1 up
1915	Onwentsia C., Lake Forest, Ill.	C. H. Vanderbeck d. W. A. Gavin	3 and 2
1916	Belmont Springs C.C., Waverley, Mass.	Alexa Stirling d. M. Caverly	2 and 1
1917-18	No tournament.		
1919	Shawnee C.C., Shawnee-on-Delaware, Pa.	Alexa Stiring d. W. A. Gavin	6 and 5
1920	Mayfield C. C., Cleveland, O.	Alexa Stirling d. J. V. Hurd	5 and 4
1921	Hollywood G.C., Deal, N.J.	Marion Hollins d. A. Stirling	5 and 4
1922	Greenbrier G.C., White Sulphur Springs, W.Va.	Glenna Collett d. W. A. Gavin	5 and 4
1923	Westchester-Biltmore C.C., Rye, N.Y.	Edith Cummings d. A. Stirling	5 and 4
1924	Rhode Island C.C., Nyatt, R.I.	Dorothy Hurd d. M. K. Browne	7 and 6
1925	St. Louis C.C., Clayton, Mo.	Glenna Collett d. W. G. Fraser	9 and 8
1926	Merion Cricket C., Haverford, Pa.	G. H. Stetson d. W. D. Gross	3 and 1
1927	Cherry Valley C., Garden City, N.Y.	M. B. Horn d. M. Orcutt	5 and 4
1928	Hot Springs (W. Va.) G.C.	Glenna Collett d. V. Van Wie	13 and 12
1929	Oakland Hills C.C., Birmingham, Mich.	Glenna Collett d. L. Pressler	4 and 3
1930	Los Angeles C.C., Beverly Hills, Cal.	Glenna Collett d. V. Van Wie	6 and 5
1931	C.C. of Buffalo, Williamsville, N.Y.	Helen Hicks d. Glenna Vare	2 and 1
1932	Salem C.C., Peabody, Mass.	Virginia Van Wie d. Glenna Vare	10 and 8
1933	Exmoor C.C., Highland Park, Ill.	Virginia Van Wie d. H. Hicks	4 and 3
1934	Whitemarsh Valley C.C., Chestnut Hill, Pa.	Virginia Van Wie d. D. Traung	2 and 1

1935	Interlachen C.C., Hopkins, Minn.	Glenna Collett Vare d. P. Berg	3 and 2
1936	Canoe Brook C.C., Summit, N.J.	Pamela Barton d. J.D. Crews	4 and 3
1937	Memphis (Tenn.) C.C.	J. A. Page, Jr. d. P. Berg	7 and 6
1938	Westmoreland Wilmette, Ill.	Patty Berg d. J.A. Page, Jr.	6 and 5
1939	Wee Burn C.C., Darien, Conn.	Betty Jameson d. D. Kirby	3 and 2
1940	Del Monte G.&C.C., Del Monte, Calif.	Betty Jameson d. J. Cochran	6 and 5
1941	The Country Club, Brookline, Mass.	Mrs. Frank Newell d. H. Sigel	5 and 3
1942-45	No tournament.		
1946	Hills C.C. Tulsa, Okla.	Mrs. George Zaharias d. C. C. Sherman	11 and 9
1947	Franklin Hills Franklin, Mich	Louise Suggs d. D. Kirby	2 up
1948	Del Monte G.&C.C., Del Monte, Calif.	Grace Lenczyk d. H. Sigel	4 and 3
1949	Merion G.C., Ardmore, Pa.	Mrs. Mark Porter d. D. Kielty	3 and 2
1950	Atlanta, A.C. Atlanta, Ga.	Beverly Hanson d. Mae Murray	6 and 4
1951	Town & C.C., St. Paul, Minn.	Dorothy Kirby d. C. Doran	2 and 1
1952	Waverley C.C., Portland, Ore.	Mrs. Jackie Pung d. S. McFedters	2 and 1
1953	Rhode Island C.C., West Barrington, R.I.	Mary Lena Faulk d. Polly Riley	3 and 2
1954	Allegheny C.C., Sewickley pa.	Barbara Romack d. M. Wright	4 and 2
1955	Myers Park C.C., Charlotte, N.C.	Pat Lesser d. J. Nelson	7 and 6
1956	Meridian Hills C.C., Indianapolis, Ind	Marlene Stewart d. J. Gunderson	2 and 1
1957	Del Paso C.C., Sacramento, Calif.	JoAnne Gunderson d. A. Johnstone	8 and 6
1958	Wee Burn C.C., Darien, Conn.	Anne Quast d. B. Romack	3 and 2
1959	Congressional C.C., Washington, D.C.	Barbara McIntire d. J. Goodwin	4 and 3
1960	Tulsa (Okla.) C.C.	JoAnne Gunderson d. Jean Ashley	6 and 5
1961	Tacoma (Wash.) C.C.	Anne Quast Decker d. Phyllis Preuss	14 and 13
1962	C.C. of Rochester, N.Y.	JoAnne Gunderson d. Ann Baker	9 and 8
1963	Taconic G.C., Williamstown, Mass.	Anne Quast Welts d. Peggy Conley	2 and 1
1964	Prairie Dunes C.C., Hutchinson, Kan.	Barbara McIntire d. JoAnne Gunderson	3 and 2

THE PROFESSIONAL GOLFERS ASSOCIATION HALL OF FAME

GOLF'S HALL OF FAME WAS ESTABLISHED BY THE PGA OF AMERICA IN 1940 TO HONOR THOSE WHO BY THEIR LIFETIME PLAYING ABILITY HAVE MADE OUTSTANDING CONTRIBUTIONS TO THE GA GAME.

A SPECIAL COMMITTEE SELECTED THE ORIGINAL GROUP OF 12 MEN FOR THE HALL OF FAME. INCLUDED IN THE 12 WERE FOUR AMATEURS.

NO ADDITIONS WERE MADE TO THE HALL OF FAME UNTIL 1953, WHEN, AT THE REQUEST OF THE PGA OF AMERICA, THE GOLF WRITERS ASSOCIATION OF AMERICA CHOSE THREE MORE MEMBERS.

IN 1954, THE PGA ESTABLISHED A NEW FORMAT FOR HALL OF FAME SELECTIONS. UNDER THIS PLAN ONE PLAYER WAS CHOSEN EACH YEAR, THAT PLAYER TO BE AT LEAST 50 YEARS OF AGE AND RETIRED FROM ACTIVE NATIONAL COMPETITION.

EACH YEAR THE PGA'S LOCAL SECTIONS WERE ASKED TO NOMINATE CANDIDATES FOR THE HALL OF FAME. THE ONE PLAYER TO BE INDUCTED EACH YEAR WAS THEN DECIDED BY A VOTE OF THE PGA MEMBERSHIP AND THOSE ON THE PGA PRESS LIST.

THAT SYSTEM REMAINED IN EFFECT THROUGH 1958. THEN THE PGA SPECIAL AWARDS COMMITTEE RECOMMENDED AND THE PGA EXECUTIVE COMMITTEE APPROVED CERTAIN MODIFICATIONS.

IN 1959, FOR THE FIRST TIME IN SIX YEARS, THREE PLAYERS WERE ELECTED TO THE HALL OF FAME IN A NATION-WIDE VOTE RESTRICTED TO PGA MEMBERS.

IN 1960, TWO PLAYERS WERE ELECTED BY THE 1959 SYSTEM. SUBSEQUENTLY, A THIRD PLAYER WAS ELECTED BY A VOTE OF THOSE ALREADY IN THE HALL OF FAME. THE SAME SYSTEM WAS USED IN THE SELECTION OF THREE NEW MEMBERS IN 1961.

IN 1962, ONE PLAYER WAS CHOSEN IN A NATION-WIDE POLL OF PGA MEMBERS AND A SECOND WAS CHOSEN, SUBSEQUENTLY, BY A VOTE OF THOSE ALREADY IN THE HALL OF FAME. THE SAME METHOD OF SELECTION WAS USED IN 1963 AND 1964.

IN 1965, THE FORMAT WAS CHANGED, WHEREBY ONLY ONE NEW MEMBER WAS ELECTED TO THE PGA HALL OF FAME. THE NEW MEMBER WAS ELECTED BY THE PRESENT LIVING MEMBERS OF THE PGA HALL OF FAME. THE SAME PROCEDURE WAS FOLLOWED IN 1966.

PLAYERS ELECTED TO THE PGA'S GOLF HALL OF FAME ARE:

1940...+WILLIE ANDERSON
TOMMY ARMOUR
+JIM BARNES
*CHICK EVANS
WALTER HAGEN
*BOB JONES
JOHN MC DERMOTT
+*FRANCIS OUIMET
GENE SARAZEN
+ALEX SMITH
*+JERRY TRAVERS
+WALTER TRAVIS

1953...BEN HOGAN
BYRON NELSON
SAM SNEAD

1954...+MACDONALD SMITH

1955...+LEO DIEGEL

1956...CRAIG WOOD

1957...DENNY SHUTE

1958...+HORTON SMITH

1959...HARRY COOPER
JOCK HUTCHISON SR.
PAUL RUNYAN

1960...MIKE BRADY
JIMMY DEMARET
FRED MC LEOD

1961...JOHNNY FARRELL
W. LAWSON LITTLE
HENRY PICARD

1962...E. J. HARRISON
OLIN DUTRA

1963...RALPH GULDAHL
JOHNNY REVOLTA

1964...LLOYD MANGRUM
+ED DUDLEY

1965...VIC GHEZZI

1966...BILLY BURKE

*AMATEURS   +DECEASED

(From the records of the Professional Golfers Association of America)

THE VARDON TROPHY AWARD

THE VARDON TROPHY

THE PGA VARDON TROPHY, NAMED IN HONOR OF THE INTERNATIONALLY FAMOUS BRITISH GOLFER, HARRY VARDON, WAS PLACED IN COMPETITION AMONG AMERICAN PROFESSIONALS IN 1937 AS A SUCCESSOR TO THE HARRY E. RADIX TROPHY, WHICH, PRIOR TO THAT TIME, HAD BEEN AWARDED ANNUALLY TO THE PROFESSIONAL HAVING THE FINEST TOURNAMENT RECORD IN COMPETITIVE PLAY IN THIS COUNTRY.

TODAY, THE VARDON TROPHY, A BRONZE COLORED PLAQUE MEASURING 39" x 27" IS AWARDED EACH YEAR TO THE MEMBER OF THE PGA OF AMERICA MAINTAINING THE FINEST PLAYING AVERAGE IN THOSE EVENTS CO-SPONSORED OR SO DESIGNATED BY THE PGA IN EACH SUCH PERIOD.

HOWEVER, SINCE THE CONCLUSION OF THE WAR, NOT ALL EVENTS ON THE PGA TOUR ARE CREDITED TOWARD THIS AWARD. IN THIS CONNECTION, IN 1947, CERTAIN INVITATIONAL EVENTS WERE EXCLUDED BY PGA TOURNAMENT REGULATIONS IN DETERMINING VARDON AWARD AND RYDER CUP TEAM STANDINGS, AND, BEGINNING WITH 1948, THE EXECUTIVE COMMITTEE OF THE PGA ADOPTED A REGULATION WHICH PROVIDES THAT THE FOLLOWING SHALL NOT BE CONSIDERED IN COMPUTING VARDON TROPHY SCORING AVERAGES, RYDER CUP TEAM POINTS AND PRIZE MONEY WINNINGS:

(A) PROFESSIONAL-AMATEUR EVENTS;
(B) INVITATIONAL EVENTS WITH FEWER THAN THIRTY (30) INVITED PLAYERS;

(C) TOURNAMENTS WHICH ARE NOT MEDAL PLAY EVENTS;

(D) ALL EVENTS WHICH ARE NOT PLAYED IN THE CONTINENTAL UNITED STATES, WITH THE EXCEPTION OF THE CANADIAN OPEN CHAMPIONSHIP; AND

(E) SECTIONAL OR LOCAL EVENTS WHICH DO NOT CARRY THE MINIMUM PURSE REQUIREMENTS OF THE PGA.

THE TOURNAMENT REGULATIONS OF THE PGA FURTHER PROVIDE THAT, FROM JANUARY 1, 1948, THROUGH DECEMBER 31, 1961, A PLAYER MUST ALSO HAVE PLAYED AT LEAST SIXTY (60) ROUNDS IN ANY ONE YEAR TO BE ELIGIBLE FOR THE VARDON AWARD IN THAT YEAR AND THAT "PICKING UP" WITHOUT THE ROUND BEING FINISHED WILL AUTOMATICALLY MAKE THE PLAYER SO DOING INELIGIBLE TO RECEIVE THE TROPHY IN THE YEAR IN WHICH SUCH HAPPENING OCCURS.

AS OF JANUARY 1, 1962, THE MINIMUM NUMBER OF OFFICIAL TOURNAMENT ROUNDS REQUIRED FOR CONSIDERATION FOR THE VARDON TROPHY HAS INCREASED TO EIGHTY (80) IN ANY ONE YEAR.

THE VARDON TROPHY HAS NOT ALWAYS BEEN AWARDED ON A BASIS OF SEASONAL PLAYING AVERAGE. FROM 1937 THROUGH 1941, THE WINNER WAS DECIDED ON A POINT BASIS. UNDER THIS SYSTEM, THE LEADING PLAYERS IN EACH EVENT RECEIVED A PRE DETERMINED NUMBER OF POINTS, AND AT THE END OF THE YEAR, THE PLAYER WITH THE GREATEST NUMBER OF POINTS WAS NAMED WAS NAMED THE WINNER.

THE VARDON TROPHY WAS NOT AWARDED FROM 1942 THROUGH 1946, DUE TO THE LIMITATIONS ON COMPETITIVE GOLF CREATED BY THE EXIGENCIES OF WORLD WAR II.

VARDON TROPHY WINNERS

YEAR	WINNER	AVERAGE	YEAR	WINNER	AVERAGE
1937	HARRY COOPER	500	1954	E. J. HARRISON	70.41
1938	SAM SNEAD	520	1955	SAM SNEAD	69.86
1939	BYRON NELSON	473	1956	CARY MIDDLECOFF	70.35
1940	BEN HOGAN	423	1957	DOW FINSTERWALD	70.30
1941	BEN HOGAN	494	1958	BOB ROSBURG	70.11
1942-1946	NO AWARD—WORLD WAR II		1959	ART WALL	70.35
1947	JIMMY DEMARET	69.90	1960	BILLY CASPER	69.950
1948	BEN HOGAN	69.30	1961	ARNOLD PALMER	69.859
1949	SAM SNEAD	69.37	1962	ARNOLD PALMER	70.271
1950	SAM SNEAD	69.23	1963	BILLY CASPER	70.588
1951	LLOYD MANGRUM	70.05	1964	ARNOLD PALMER	70.010
1952	JACK BURKE	70.54	1965	BILLY CASPER	70.586
1953	LLOYD MANGRUM	70.22	1966	BILLY CASPER	70.276

(From the records of the Professional Golfers Association of America)

PRIZE MONEY AWARDED IN NATIONAL PGA CHAMPIONSHIPS

PGA CHAMPIONSHIP DOLLAR SUMMARY

Year	Winner	Played at	First Place Prize Money	Total Prize Money
1916	James M. Barnes	Siwanoy Country Club, Bronxville, N.Y.		$ 2,580.00
1917-1918 (No Championship Played)				
1919	James M. Barnes	Engineers Country Club, Roslyn, L.I., N.Y.		*
1920	Jock Hutchison	Flossmoor Country Club, Flossmoor, Ill.		*
1921	Walter Hagen	Inwood Country Club, Far Rockaway, N.Y.		2,580.00
1922	Gene Sarazen	Oakmont Country Club, Oakmont, Pa.		*

Year	Winner	Site		
1923	Gene Sarazen	Pelham Country Club, Pelham, N.Y.		*
1924	Walter Hagen	French Lick Country Club, French Lick, Ind.		6,830.00
1925	Walter Hagen	Olympia Fields Country Club, Olympia Fields, Ill.		6,330.00
1926	Walter Hagen	Salisbury Golf Club, Westbury, L.I., N.Y.		11,100.00
1927	Walter Hagen	Cedar Crest Country Club, Dallas, Texas		15,441.05
1928	Leo Diegel	Five Farms Country Club, Baltimore, Md.		10,400.00
1929	Leo Diegel	Hillcrest Country Club, Los Angeles, Calif.		5,000.00
1930	Tommy Armour	Fresh Meadows Country Club, Flushing, N.Y.		10,300.00
1931	Tom Creavy	Wannamoisett Country Club, Rumford, R. I.	Records not Available	7,200.00
1932	Olin Dutra	Keller Golf Club, St. Paul, Minn.		7,200.00
1933	Gene Sarazen	Blue Mound Country Club, Milwaukee, Wis.		7,200.00
1934	Paul Runyan	Park Country Club, Williamsville, N.Y.		7,200.00
1935	Johnny Revolta	Twin Hills Country Club, Oklahoma City, Okla.		7,820.00
1936	Denny Shute	Pinehurst Country Club, Pinehurst, N.C.		9,200.00
1937	Denny Shute	Pittsburgh Field Club, Aspinwall, Pa.		9,200.00
1938	Paul Runyan	Shawnee Country Club, Shawnee-on-Delaware, Pa.		10,000.00
1939	Henry Picard	Pomonok Country Club, Flushing, L.I., N.Y.		10,600.00
1940	Byron Nelson	Hershey Country Club, Hershey, Pa.		11,050.00
1941	Vic Ghezzi	Cherry Hills Country Club, Denver, Colo.		10,600.00
1942	Sam Snead	Seaview Country Club, Atlantic City, N.J.		7,550.00
1943	(No Championship Played)			—
1944	Bob Hamilton	Manito Golf & Country Club, Spokane, Wash.	$ 3,500	14,500.00
1945	Byron Nelson	Morraine Country Club, Dayton, Ohio	3,750	14,700.00
1946	Ben Hogan	Portland Golf Club, Portland, Ore.	3,500	17,700.00
1947	Jim Ferrier	Plum Hollow Country Club, Detroit, Mich.	3,500	17,700.00
1948	Ben Hogan	Norwood Hills Country Club, St. Louis, Mo.	3,500	17,700.00
1949	Sam Snead	Hermitage Country Club, Richmond, Va.	3,500	17,700.00
1950	Chandler Harper	Scioto Country Club, Columbus, Ohio	3,500	17,700.00
1951	Sam Snead	Oakmont Country Club, Oakmont, Pa.	3,500	17,700.00
1952	Jim Turnesa	Big Spring Country Club, Louisville, Ky.	3,500	17,700.00
1953	Walter Burkemo	Birmingham Country Club, Birmingham, Mich.	5,000	20,700.00
1954	Chick Harbert	Keller Golf Club, St. Paul, Minn.	5,000	20,700.00
1955	Doug Ford	Meadowbrook Country Club, Detroit, Mich.	5,000	20,700.00
1956	Jack Burke	Blue Hill Country Club, Boston, Mass.	5,000	40,000.00
1957	Lionel Hebert	Miami Valley Golf Club, Dayton, Ohio	8,000	42,100.00
1958	Dow Finsterwald**	Llanerch Country Club, Havertown, Pa.	5,500	39,400.00
1959	Bob Rosburg	Minneapolis Golf Club, St. Louis Park, Minn.	8,250	51,175.00
1960	Jay Herbert	Firestone Country Club, Akron, Ohio	11,000	63,130.00
1961	Jerry Barber	Olympia Fields Country Club, Olympia Fields, Ill.	11,000	64,800.00
1962	Gary Player	Aronimink Golf Club, Newtown Square, Pa.	13,000	72,500.00
1963	Jack Nicklaus	Dallas Athletic Club Country Club, Dallas, Texas	13,000	80,900.00
1964	Bob Nichols	Columbus Country Club, Columbus, Ohio	18,000	100,000.00
1965	Dave Marr	Laural Valley Golf Club, Ligonier, Pa.	25,000	149,700.00
1966	Al Geiberger	Firestone Country Club, Akron, Ohio	25,000	150,000.00
1967	Don January	Columbine Country Club, Denver, Colo.	25,000	150,000.00

*No record available.
**Match to medal play.

(From the records of the Professional Golfers Association of America)

All-Time

Official Money Winners

From 1947 Through 1966

Individual Accumulative PGA Official Earnings

1.	Arnold Palmer	$754,450.15
2.	Billy Casper	593,944.09
3.	Jack Nicklaus	527,364.75
4.	Julius Boros	442,235.99
5.	Gene Littler	441,025.66
6.	Doug Sanders	379,668.01
7.	Gary Player	365,090.11
8.	Sam Snead	363,423.20
9.	Doug Ford	360,284.46
10.	Tony Lema	352,095.09
11.	Dow Finsterwald	333,602.05
12.	Cary Middlecoff	294,168.33
13.	Art Wall	290,555.29
14.	Jay Hebert	273,848.31
15.	Mike Souchak	273,720.26
16.	Bobby Nichols	270,857.92
17.	Ted Kroll	258,996.94
18.	Don January	257,330.19
19.	Jack Burke	253,232.22
20.	Tommy Bolt	251,225.61
21.	Al Geiberger	248,583.78
22.	Johnny Pott	248,408.40
23.	Billy Maxwell	246,161.63
24.	Mason Rudolph	243,449.88
25.	Ken Venturi	242,505.27

(From the records of the Professional Golfers
Association of America)

Annual Leading Money Winners

Leading Money Winners (1934-1966)

1934 --	Paul Runyan.....................	$ 6,767.00
1935 --	Johnny Revolta	9,543.00
1936 --	Horton Smith.................	7,682.00
1937 --	Harry Cooper	14,138.69
1938 --	Sam Snead....................	19,534.49
1939 --	Henry Picard	10,303.00
1940 --	Ben Hogan	10,655.00
1941 --	Ben Hogan	18,358,00
1942 --	Ben Hogan	13,143.00
1943 --	No Statistics Compiled	
1944 --	Byron Nelson. (War Bonds)	37,967.69
1945 --	Byron Nelson. (War Bonds)	63,335.66
1946 --	Ben Hogan	42,556.16
1947 --	Jimmy Demaret...............	27,936.83
1948 --	Ben Hogan	32,112.00
1949 --	Sam Snead	31,593.83
1950 --	Sam Snead	35,758.83
1951 --	Lloyd Mangrum...............	26,088.83
1952 --	Julius Boros	37,032.97
1953 --	Lew Worsham	34,002.00
1954 --	Bob Toski....................	65,819.81
1955 --	Julius Boros	63,121.55
1956 --	Ted Kroll	72,835.83
1957 --	Dick Mayer..................	65,835.00
1958 --	Arnold Palmer	42,607.50
1959 --	Art Wall, Jr.	52,167.60
1960 -	Arnold Palmer	75,262.85
1961 --	Gary Player	64,540.45
1962 --	Arnold Palmer	81,448.33
1963 --	Arnold Palmer	128,230.00
1964 --	Jack Nicklaus	113,284.50
1965 --	Jack Nicklaus	140,752.14
1966 --	Billy Casper	121,944.92
1967 --	Arnold Palmer	182,393.96 (To 10-1-67)

(From the records of the Professional Golfers Association of America)

Ladies Annual Leading Money Winners

(From 1948 through 1966)

Year	Player	Money
1948	Babe Zaharias	$ 3,400
1949	Babe Zaharias	4,650
1950	Babe Zaharias	14,800
1951	Babe Zaharias	15,087
1952	Betsy Rawls	14,505
1953	Louise Suggs	19,816

1954

Player	Money
1. Patty Berg	$16,011
2. Babe Zaharias	14,452
3. Louise Suggs	12,736
4. Betsy Rawls	8,852
5. Betty Jameson	8,749
6. Betty Hicks	7,054
7. Beverly Hanson	6,415
8. Jackie Pung	6,291
9. Betty Dodd	6,277
10. Fay Crocker	5,270

1955

Player	Money
1. Patty Berg	$16,497
2. Louise Suggs	13,729
3. Fay Crocker	12,679
4. Betty Jameson	10,699
5. Mary L. Faulk	10,390
6. Beverly Hanson	10,338
7. Jackie Pung	9,259
8. Betty Hicks	8,334
9. Marlene Bauer	7,051
10. Betsy Rawls	6,967

1956

Player	Money
1. Marlene Hagge	$20,235
2. Patty Berg	12,560
3. Louise Suggs	12,434
4. Fay Crocker	10,107
5. Joyce Ziske	9,733
6. Betty Jameson	9,056
7. Mickey Wright	8,253
8. Kathy Cornelius	7,336
9. Mary Lena Faulk	7,077
10. Beverly Hanson	7,032

1957

Player	Money
1. Patty Berg	$16,272
2. Fay Crocker	12,019
3. Mickey Wright	11,131
4. Marlene Hagge	10,260
5. Wiffi Smith	10,251
6. Betsy Rawls	9,812
7. Louise Suggs	9,207
8. Betty Dodd	8,570
9. Beverly Hanson	7,073
10. Betty Jameson	7,017

1958

Player	Money
1. Betty Hanson	$12,639
2. Marlene Hagge	11,890
3. Louise Suggs	11,862
4. Mickey Wright	11,775
5. Fay Crocker	11,570
6. Jackie Pung	8,493
7. Patty Berg	8,014
8. Betsy Rawls	7,600
9. Mary L. Faulk	7,290

1959

Player	Money
1. Betsy Rawls	$26,774
2. Mickey Wright	18,182
3. Louise Suggs	16,936
4. Bev Hanson	14,018
5. Marlene Hagge	12,056
6. Patty Berg	11,495
7. Joyce Ziske	11,452
8. Fay Crocker	9,667
9. Mary Lena Faulk	9,150
10. Bonnie Randolph	8,578

1960

Player	Money
1. Louise Suggs	$16,892
2. Mickey Wright	16,380
3. Betsy Rawls	14,928
4. Joyce Ziske	12,886
5. Fay Crocker	12,128
6. Mary Lena Faulk	9,629
7. Wiffi Smith	9,265
8. Patty Berg	9,019
9. Kathy Cornelius	8,886
10. Marlene Hagge	7,212

1961

Player	Money
1. Mickey Wright	$22,236
2. Betsy Rawls	15,672
3. Louise Suggs	15,339
4. Mary Lena Faulk	12,968

5.	Marilynn Smith	10,687
6.	Ruth Jessen	9,886
7.	Barbara Romack	8,895
8.	Marlene Hagge	8,245
9.	Jo Ann Prentice	8,162
10.	Kathy Cornelius	7,915

1962

Player		Money
1.	Mickey Wright	$21,641
2.	Kathy Whitworth	17,044
3.	Mary Lena Faulk	14,949
4.	Ruth Jessen	14,937
5.	Marilynn Smith	12,075
6.	Shirley Engelhorn	11,719
7.	Patty Berg	10,682
8.	Betsy Rawls	10,428
9.	Jo Ann Prentice	9,184
10.	Barbara Romack	8,639

1963

Player		Money
1.	Mickey Wright	$31,269
2.	Kathy Whitworth	26,858
3.	Marilynn Smith	21,691
4.	Betsy Rawls	17,864
5.	Clifford Ann Creed	13,843
6.	Sandra Haynie	13,683
7.	Marlene Hagge	13,570
8.	Shirley Englehor	13,082
9.	Ruth Jessen	10,777
10.	Jo Ann Prentice	9,401

1964

Player		Money
1.	Mickey Wright	$29,800
2.	Ruth Jessen	23,431
3.	Kathy Whitworth	20,434
4.	Betsy Rawls	19,350
5.	Marlene Hagge	18,843
6.	Shirley Englehorn	18,582
7.	Sandra Haynie	17,061
8.	Clifford Ann Creed	15,443
9.	Mary Mills	13,963
10.	Marilynn Smith	12,738

1965

Player		Money
1.	Kathy Whitworth	$28,658
2.	Marlene Hagge	21,532
3.	Carol Mann	20,875
4.	Clifford Ann Creed	20,795
5.	Sandra Haynie	17,722
6.	Marilynn Smith	16,692
7.	Mary Mills	13,007
8.	Susie Maxwell	12,982
9.	Judy Torluemke	12,237
10.	Betsy Rawls	10,898

1966

Player		Money
1.	Kathy Whitworth	$33,517
2.	Sandra Haynie	30,157
3.	Mickey Wright	26,672
4.	Carol Mann	23,246
5.	Clifford Ann Creed	21,089

Notes

1. Andrew Lang, *The Badminton Library*, Longmans, Green & Co. 1890.
2. John Kerr, *The Golf-Book of East Lothian*, T. A. Constable, 1896.
3. James Grierson, *Delineations of St. Andrews*, Cupar, 1833.
4. James Lindsey Stewart, *Golfiana Miscellanea*, Hamilton Adams Inc., 1887.
5. Sir Walter G. Simpson, *The Art Of Golf*, 1887.
6. Horace G. Hutchinson, *Sports & Pastimes*, Longmans, Green & Co., 1895.
7. H. B. Farnie, *The Golfer's Manual*, The Dropmore Press, 1857.
8. Robert Clark, *Golf, A Royal and Ancient Game*, MacMillan & Co., 1875.
9. H. S. C. Everard, *History of the Royal and Ancient G. C.*, Blackwood, 1907.
10. W. E. Hughes, *Chronicles of the Blackheath Golfers*, Chapman & Hill, 1897.
11. Thomas Aitchison & George Lorimer, *Bruntsfield Links G. C.*, 1902.
12. Robert Clark, *Golf, A Royal & Ancient Game*, MacMillan & Co., 1875.
13. H. G. Hutchinson, *British Golf Links*, J. S. Virtue & Co., 1897.
14. James G. Dow, *The Crail Golfing Society*, Edinburgh, 1936.
15. Charles Smith, *The Aberdeen Golfers*, Privately, 1896.
16. James Colville, *Glasgow Golf Club*, 1787-1907, John Smith, 1907.
17. Henry Farnie, *Handy-book of the Fife Coast*, Cupar-Fife, No Date.
18. Bernard Darwin, *History of Golf in Great Britain*, Cassell & Co., 1952.
19. Peter Baxter, *Golf in Perth and Perthshire*, Hunter, 1899.
20. Henry B. Farnie, *The Golfers Manual*, Dropmore Press, 1857.
21. T. D. Miller, *Famous Scottish Links*, R. & R. Clark, Ltd., Edinburgh, 1911.
22. James E. Shaw, *Prestwick Golf Club*, Jackson & Sons, 1938.
23. William Caw, *King James VI Golf Club*, R. & R. Clark, Ltd., 1912.
24. H. S. C. Everard, *History of the Royal & Ancient G. C. of St. Andrews*, 1907.
25. Horace G. Hutchinson, *British Golf Links*, Virtue & Co., 1897.
26. Robert Clark, *Golf, A Royal & Ancient Game*, MacMillan & Co., 1875.
27. The Rev. J. G. McPherson, *Golf and Golfers Past and Present*, 1891.
28. D. S. Salmond, *Reminiscences of Arbroath & St. Andrews*, Arbroath, 1905.
29. James Lindsay Stewart, *Golfiana Miscellanea*, Glasgow, 1887.
30. John Kerr, *The Golf Book Of East Lothian*, T. & A. Constable, 1896.
31. W. W. Tullock, *The Life Of Tom Morris*, T. Werner Laurie, 1908.
32. James Balfour, *Golf On St. Andrews Links, Reminiscences of Golf*, Edinburgh: David Douglas, 1887.
33. H. S. C. Everard, *History of the Royal & Ancient G. C. of St. Andrews*, 1907.
34. James E. Shaw, *Prestwick Golf Club*, Jackson and Sons, 1938.
35. Charles G. Mortimer & Fred Pignon, *The Open Championship*, Jarrolds, London Ltd., 1952.
36. William R. Chambers, *Golfing*, Edinburgh, & London, 1887.
37. Andrew Kirkaldy, *Fifty Years of Golf*, T. Fisher Unwin Ltd., 1921.
38. W. W. Tulloch, *The Life of Tom Morris*, T. Werner Laurie, 1907.
39. *The Goff. Heroi-Comical Poem.* In Three Cantos. Second Edition. Edinburgh: Printed for Peter Hill. 1793.
40. Peter Lawless, *The Golfer's Companion*, J. M. Dent, London, 1937.
41. Guy B. Farrar, *Royal Liverpool Golf Club*, Wilmer Bros., & Co., 1933.
42. Peter Lawless, *The Golfers Companion*, J. M. Dent & Sons, Ltd., 1937.
43. Guy B. Farrar, *Royal Liverpool Golf Club*, Wilmer Bros., & Co., 1933.
44. Peter Lawless, *Golfers Companion*, J. M. Dent & Sons, 1937.
45. Andra Kirkaldy, *Fifty Years Of Golf*, T. Fisher Unwin, Ltd., 1921.
(This Is the First Golf Book Published in the U.S.)
46. James P. Lee, *Golf*, Dodd, Mead & Co., 1895.
47. H. B. Martin, *Fifty Years of American Golf*, Dodd, Mead & Co., 1933.
48. Don Weis, *United States Golf Asso., Journal*, February Issue, 1964.

49. Bernard Darwin, *Golf — Pleasures of Life Series*, Burke, London, 1954.
50. H. B. Martin, *Fifty Years of American Golf*, Dodd, Mead & Co., 1936.
51. Charles B. Macdonald, *Scotland's Gift Golf*, Charles Scribner's Sons, 1928.
52. Herbert Warren Wind, *The Story of American Golf*, Farrar, Straus & Co., 1948.
53. Nevin H. Gibson, *The Encyclopedia of Golf*, A. S. Barnes & Co., 1958 & 1964.
54. Issette Pearson, *The Ladies Golf Union Official Year Book*.
55. D. M. Mathison, *The Golfers Handbook*, Edinburgh, Scotland.
56. May Hezlet, *Ladies Golf*, Hutchinson & Co., 1904.
57. Mabel Springer, *Golfing Reminiscences*, Mills & Boon Ltd., 1924.
58. *Golf, Great Britain*, Vol. XI, London, England, 1895.
59. H. B. Martin, *Fifty Years of American Golf*, Dodd, Mead & Co., 1936.
60. Charles B. Macdonald, *Scotland's Golf of Golf*, Charles Scribner & Sons, 1928.
61. Herbert Warren Wind, *The Story of American Golf*, Farrar, Straus & Co., 1948.
62. Havemeyer trophy later destroyed by fire at East Lake C. C. Bobby Jones won it in 1924 and 1925. It was replaced by the U.S.G.A.
63. *United States Golf Association Record Book*, 1953.
64. The Record Books from each association.
65. John L. Low, *The Golfers' Year-Book*, London, James Nisbet & Co.
66. H. B. Martin, *Fifty Years of American Golf*, Dodd, Mead & Co., 1936.
67. Bernard Darwin, *Playing the Like*, Sportsman Book Club, 1952.
68. Nevin H. Gibson, *The Encyclopedia of Golf*, A. S. Barnes & Co., 1958.
69. Robert Browning, *A History of Golf*, J. M. Dent & Sons, 1955.
70. Grantland Rice, *The American Golfer*.
71. Jerome D. Travers & James R. Crowell, *The Fifth Estate*, A. Knopp, 1926.
72. Bernard Darwin, *From Out of the Rough*, London, 1932.
73. P. J. Boatwright, Jr. *Professional Golfer* Magazine, July 1967.
74. Henry Leach, *American Golfer* Magazine, October Issue, 1913.
75. Francis Ouimet, *A Game of Golf*, Hutchinson & Co., 1933.
76. Herbert Warren Wind, *The Story of American Golf*, Farrar, Straus, 1948.
77. John H. Taylor, *My Life's Work*, Golf. Jonathan Cape, 1943.
78. Bernard Darwin, *Green Memories*, Hodder & Stoughton, 1933.
79. Jerome D. Travers, *The Fifth Estate*, Alfred A. Knopp, 1926.
80. United States Golf Association Year Book of 1921.
81. *USGA Record Book of Championships 1895 through 1953*, 1954.
82. *USGA Record Book of Championships 1895 through 1953*.
83. Gene Sarazen, *Thirty Years of Championship Golf*, Prentice Hall, 1950.
84. Joyce Wethered, *Golfing Memories & Methods*, Mayflower Press, 1933.
85. Robert T. Jones, Jr., *Down The Fairway*, Mintonm Balch & Co., N. Y., 1927.
86. *PGA Tournament Record Book*, 1949.
87. O. B. Keeler, *Boys' Life of Bobby Jones*, Harper & Brothers, 1931.
88. Grantland Rice, *The Tumult and the Shouting*, A. S. Barnes & Co., 1954.
89. Gene Sarazen, *Thirty Years of Championship Golf*, Prentice-Hall, 1950.
90. Grantland Rice, *The Tumult and the Shouting*, A. S. Barnes & Co., 1954.
91. Henry Cotton, *This Game of Golf*, Country Life, 1948.
92. George Duncan, *Golf at A Gallop*, Sporting Handbooks, Ltd., 1951.
93. Nevin H. Gibson, *The Encyclopedia of Golf*, A. S. Barnes & Co., 1958.
94. *The Golfer's Handbook*, Edinburgh, Scotland (British) 1949.
95. H. B. Martin, *Fifty Years of American Golf*, Dodd, Mead & Co., 1936.
96. Lillian Harlow, *Golf World Magazine*, Southern Pines, N. C.
97. *U.S.G.A. Record Books*, 1932 through 1936.
98. *P.G.A. Twentieth Annual Meeting Booklet*, 1936.
99. Richardson and Werden, The 1932 *Yearbook*.
100. *U.S.G.A. Record Book*, 1936.
101. Tom Flaherty, *The Masters*, Holt, Rinehart & Winston, 1961.
102. Herbert Warren Wind, *The Complete Golfer*, Simon & Schuster, 1954.
103. *U.S.G.A. Year Book*, 1938.
104. *P.G.A. Tournament Record Book*, 1949.
105. Herbert Warren Wind, *The Story of American Golf*, Farrar & Straus Co., 1948.
106. Ed Dudley, *P.G.A. Annual Report of 1946*.
107. *U.S.G.A. Year Book*, 1949.
108. Geoffrey Cousins, *Golfers At Law*, Alfred A. Knopf, 1959.
109. Snead has won every major championship except the U.S. Open, although he has been a runner-up on four occasions.
110. Nevin H. Gibson, *The Encyclopedia of Golf*, A. S. Barnes & Co., 1958 & 1964.
111. Nevin H. Gibson, *The Encyclopedia of Golf*, A. S. Barnes & Co., 1964.
112. United States Golf Association. *Record Book of Championships 1895–1953*.
113. Fred Corcoran, *International Golf Association's Report*.
114. *United States Golf Association Year Book* of 1954.
115. *United States Golf Association Year Book*, 1954.
116. *United States Golf Association Year Book*, 1955
117. *U.S.G.A. 1955 Supplement to the Record Book of Championships*.
118. See statistical chart on golf courses.
119. *USGA Championships and International Events Record Book*, 1895 thru 1961.
120. *PGA Tournament Record Book of 1960*.
121. *National Golf Foundation Report*. Annual Report for 1960.
122. *Golf Digest* Magazine. Annual Issue of 1961.
123. *Professional Golfers* Magazine.
124. *Golf World* Magazine.
125. *National Golf Foundation Annual Report*.
126. Ladies Professional Golf Association and the National Golf Foundation.
127. National Golf Foundation. Annual Report of 1964.
128. Athletic Goods Manufacturing Association Report of 1965.
129. *Golf Digest 1965 Annual* Magazine.
130. Ken's great recovery has induced the film industry to produce a motion picture on his life, *Comeback*.
131. National Golf Foundation, Chicago, Ill.
132. *Golf World* Magazine, Southern Pines, N. C.
133. *Athletic Goods Manufacturers Association Census Report for 1965*.
134. *Golf World* Magazine, Southern Pines, N. C.
135. Nevin H. Gibson, *Golf News*, San Francisco, Cal.
136. The Professional Golfers Association of America Records Book.
137. National Golf Foundation Statistics of 1966, Chicago, Ill.

138. While returning from the PGA on the Ohio Turnpike I heard of Tony's death on the radio. It seemed that I had just spoken to him ten minutes ago and I had to stop and comprehend this terrible tragedy. "Champagne" Tony was a friend of every fellow pro, spectator, and, particularly, the golf writers. On every victory he purchased champagne for the press, thus his name was coined, 'Champagne Tony.'

His departure is a great loss to the golfing world.

139. Maury Fitzgerald, *The Washington Post*, Wash., D.C.

140. *Golf* Magazine, New York, N. Y.

141. Joe C. Dey, Jr., *The USGA Journal*, July 1967.

142. Ron Coffman, *Golf World* Magazine, July 7, 1967.

143. T. R. Clougher, *Golf Clubs of the Empire*, London, 1928.

Index